MEMOIRS

OF THE LATE

THOMAS HOLCROFT.

VOL. I.

Blood Sculp^t

Thomas Holcroft

London Published for Longman & Co. April 6th 1816.

MEMOIRS

OF THE LATE

THOMAS HOLCROFT,

Written by Himself,

AND CONTINUED

TO THE TIME OF HIS DEATH,

FROM HIS DIARY,

NOTES, AND OTHER PAPERS.

IN THREE VOLUMES.

VOL. I.

London:

PRINTED FOR LONGMAN, HURST, REES, ORME, AND BROWN, PATERNOSTER-ROW.

1816.

J. M'Creery, Printer,
Black-Horse-Court, London.

ADVERTISEMENT.

Mr. Holcroft had intended, for several years before his death, to write an account of his own life. It is now only to be regretted that he did not begin to execute this design sooner. Few lives have been marked with more striking changes; and no one possessed the qualities necessary for describing them with characteristic liveliness in a greater degree than he did. It often happens, that what we most wish done, we fail to do, either through fear lest the execution should not answer our expectations, or because the pleasure with which we contemplate a favourite object at a distance, makes us neglect the ordinary means of attaining it. This seems to have been the case with Mr. Holcroft, who did not begin the work he had so long projected, till within a short time of his death. How much he had it at heart, may however be inferred from the extraordinary pains he then took to make some progress in it. He told his physicians that he did not care what severity of treatment he was subjected to, provided he could live six months longer to complete what he had begun. By dictating a word at a time, he succeeded in bringing it down to his fifteenth year. When the clearness, minuteness, and vividness of what he thus wrote, are compared with the feeble, half-convulsed state in which it was written, it will be difficult to bring a stronger instance of the exertion of resolution and firmness of mind, under such circumstances. The whole of this account is given literally to the public. This part comprises the first seventeen Chapters, or Book I. The remainder of the Life has been compiled from Mr. Holcroft's Letters; from Journals and other papers to which I had access; from conversations with some of his early and most intimate friends; and from passages in his printed works, relating to his own history and adventures, pointed out to me by them. Some of the anecdotes I have also heard mentioned by himself; but these are comparatively few. I first became acquainted with Mr. Holcroft about ten years ago; my chief intercourse with him was within the last three or four years of his life.

WM. HAZLITT.

January, 1810.

THE LIFE

OF

THOMAS HOLCROFT.

BOOK I.

CHAP. I.

[*This and the remaining Chapters of the first Book are in Mr. Holcroft's own words.*]

"I WAS born in London, in Orange Court, Leicester Fields, on the 10th day of December, 1745, old style; and was baptized and registered in St. Martin's church, where my name is erroneously written Howlcroft. In a will of one of my uncle's, which may be seen in Doctors' Commons, the name is spelt Houldecroft. From this it appears that our family did not pay much attention to subjects of orthography, or think the manner in which their name was spelt, a matter of importance.

Most persons, I believe, retain through life, a few strong impressions of very early childhood. I have a recollection of being played with by my parents, when very young, and of the extreme pleasure it gave me. On another occasion, as I and one or two of my brothers or sisters were playing in the court, and kneeling and peeping down a cellar window, where there were some fowls, a shutter that belonged to the window, and was fastened up, by some means or other got loose, and entirely cut off one side of my sister Anne's thumb;—a disaster never afterwards to be forgotten. My father one day whipped me very severely for crying to go to a school in the neighbourhood, where children were sent rather to keep them out of the way, than to learn any thing. He afterwards ordered an apprentice he had to take me to school. This apprentice was an exceedingly hard-featured youth, with thick lips, wide mouth, broad nose, and his face very much marked with the small-pox, but very kind and good tempered. I perfectly remember his carrying me in my petticoats, consoling me as we went, and giving me something nice to eat. Perhaps I bear his features in mind the more accurately, because I occasionally saw him afterwards, till I was seven or eight years old, when he used to visit my father, who was then under misfortunes. He seldom came without something kind to say, or good to give: but his last and capital gift, too precious to be ever forgotten, consisted of two small books. One was the History of Parismus and Parismenes, and the other, of the Seven Champions of Christendom. These were to me an inestimable treasure, that often brought the rugged, good natured Dick to my remembrance, with no slight sense of obligation.

Till I was about six years old, my father kept a shoe-maker's shop in Orange Court; and I have a faint recollection that my mother dealt in greens and oysters. After I became a man, my father more than once pointed out the house to me: the back of it looks into the King's Mews, and it is now No. 13. My father was fond of speculation, and very adventurous. I believe he had been set up in trade by my uncle John, who lived several years, first as a helper, and afterwards as a groom in the King's stables; where, being an excellent economist, he saved money. For a time, my father, through John's influence, was admitted a helper in the stables; but he did not continue there long, not having his brother's perseverance. How or when he procured the little knowledge of shoemaking which he had, I do not recollect; though I have heard him mention the fact. He was not bred to the trade. He and a numerous family of his brothers and sisters all spent their infancy in *the field country*; or, as I have heard him describe it, the most desolate part of Lancashire, called Martin's Muir, where my grand-father was a cooper; a man, according to my father's account, possessed of good qualities, but passionate, and a dear lover of Sir John Barleycorn. My grandmother was always mentioned by my father with very great respect.

At the period of which I speak, the west end of London swarmed with chairmen; who, that they might tread more safely, had their shoes made differently from those of other people; to which particular branch of the trade my father applied himself with some success. But he was not satisfied with the profits he acquired by shoe-making: he was very fond of horses, and having some knowledge of them, he became a dealer in them. Few persons but the great, at this time kept any sort of carriage. It was common for those who wished to ride out, to hire a horse for the day; and my father kept several horses for this purpose. If his word was to be taken, they were such as were not very easily to be matched. The praise he bestowed on them for their performances, and his admiration of their make and beauty, were strong and continued. Young as I was, he earnestly wished to see me able to ride. He had a beautiful poney (at least so he called, and so I thought, it): but it was not more remarkable for its beauty, than its animation. To hold it, required all my father's strength and skill; yet he was determined I should mount this poney, and accompany him, whenever he took a ride. For this purpose my petticoats were discarded; and as he was fonder of me than even of his horses, nay, or of his poney, he had straps made, and I was buckled to the saddle, with a leading rein fastened to the muzzle of the poney, which he carefully held. These rides, with the oddity of our equipage and appearance, sometimes exposed us to the ridicule of bantering acquaintance; but I remember no harm that happened.

About the same time, my father indulged another whim; whether he was led to it by any particular accident, I cannot tell. I must have been about five years old, when he put me under the tuition of a player on the violin, who was a public performer of some repute. Either parental fondness led my father to believe, or he was flattered into the supposition, that I had an uncommon aptitude for the art I had been put to learn. I shall never forget the high praises I received, the affirmation that I was a prodigy, and the assurances my teachers gave that I should soon be heard in public. These dreams were never realized.

My father was under great obligations to my uncle John, and was afraid, especially just at that time, of disobliging him. My uncle's pride took the alarm; and after marking his disapprobation, he asked with contempt, "Do you mean to make a fiddler of the boy?" My practice on the violin therefore ceased; and it is perhaps worth remarking, that, though I could play so well before I was six years old, I had wholly forgotten the art at the age of seven; for, after my master left me, I never touched the instrument. In the days of my youthful distress, I have sometimes thought, with bitter regret, of the absurd pride of my uncle.

CHAP. II.

"THUS far my infantine life had passed under much more favourable circumstances than are common to the children of the poor. But, when I was about six years old, the scene suddenly changed, a long train of increasing hardships began, and I have no doubt my sufferings were rendered more severe from a consciousness of the little I had suffered till then. This may therefore be properly considered as the first remarkable era in my life.

How far the state of my father's affairs might contribute to the steps he took, is more than I now can tell: but on a sudden the house-keeping broke up, the horses were sold, and we went into Berkshire, somewhere beyond Ascot Heath, about thirty miles from London, where my father had taken a house. What became of his effects, in what manner they were sold, and of every circumstance of that kind, I am totally ignorant.

I suppose the time of our residence in Berkshire to have been about twelve months. The house where we lived, was situated at the corner of the road, the last of a small Green, or Common, down which the road had a descent. For I remember my father at first had a tall, high-boned hack, on the bare back of which I used by his order to gallop down the hill, though I felt great difficulty in keeping my seat.

It was in this retired spot that my father himself began to teach me to read. The task at first I found difficult, till the idea one day suddenly seized me of catching all the sounds I had been taught from the arrangement of the letters; and my joy at this amazing discovery was so great, that the recollection of it has never been effaced. After that, my progress was so rapid, that it astonished my father. He boasted of me to every body; and that I might lose no time, the task he set me was eleven chapters a day in the Old Testament. I might indeed have deceived my father by skipping some of the chapters, but a dawning regard for truth, aided by the love I had of reading, and the wonderful histories I sometimes found in the Sacred Writings, generally induced me to go through the whole of my task. One day as I was sitting at the gate with my Bible in my hand, a neighbouring farmer, coming to see my father, asked me if I could read the Bible already? I answered, yes; and he desired me to let him hear me. I began at the place where the book was open, read fluently, and afterwards told him, that if he pleased, he should hear the tenth chapter of Nehemiah. At this he seemed still more amazed, and wishing to be convinced, bade me read. After listening till he found I could really pronounce the uncouth Hebrew names so much better and more easily than he supposed to be within the power of so young a child, he patted my head, gave me a penny, and said I was an uncommon boy. It would be hard to say whether his praise or his gift was most flattering to me. Soon after, my father's apprentice, the kind-hearted Dick, who came backward and forward to my father on his affairs, brought me the two delightful histories I have above-mentioned, which were among those then called Chapman's Books. It was scarcely possible for any thing to have been more grateful to me than this present. Parismus and Parismenes, with all the adventures detailed in the Seven Champions of Christendom, were soon as familiar to me as my catechism, or the daily prayers I repeated kneeling before my father. Oh, how I loved poor Dick!

My father was an excellent pedestrian, and would often walk to London and back again, more than sixty miles, in the same day. Sometimes he dined at home, and went to London in the afternoon; and even then, I rather think, though I cannot be certain, that he made a point of sleeping in his own house. In height he was about five feet four, perfectly free from corpulency, sober, and satisfied with plain, wholesome diet. He used to speak with great self-complacency of the manner in which he overcame competitors in walking, with whom he sometimes chanced to meet. "I have been overtaken by tall men," he would say, "with whom I could not keep pace, and they have bid me good bye, and told me they should be in London at such a time before me: but they were every one of them mistaken. They could not proceed without stopping to rest, and taking their pint of beer, their bread and cheese, or whatever they could get to eat and drink. I was never far behind them, I wanted nothing to eat or drink, I was not weary, I passed the houses in which they were sitting, and got forward sometimes more than a mile before them; while they would make another call, perhaps, and another, so that I always arrived before them."

One afternoon, however, he was desirous of going to town at a later hour than usual, and therefore, for expedition's sake, he borrowed a light grey horse of a neighbour, on condition that it should be returned that evening. He then mounted, and placed me behind him, trusting to my courage and good sense for finding my way home with the horse. I know not how far he took me, except that we passed over some part of Ascot Heath, if not all of it; and about an hour before it was dark, he alighted, left me on horse-back, and carefully gave me such directions as he supposed I could not mistake. In this he conjectured rightly; I began to trot away, anxious to get home before it was too dark; but unluckily for me, some time after we had parted, with no human being in sight, nor any likelihood of meeting one, the horse stumbled among some ruts, and threw my hat off. To have lost my hat would have been a terrible misfortune; I therefore ventured to alight and pick it up. Then it was that I perceived my distress. I found every attempt I made to remount wholly ineffectual, and all I could do was to endeavour to drag the sluggish animal along, and cry bitterly. Twilight was fast approaching, and I alone on the heath, (I knew not how far from home), and never expecting to reach that desired place that evening. At length, however, the white railing of the Race Course on Ascot Heath came in sight, and I conceived hopes of remounting. Accordingly I with great difficulty prevailed on my grey nag to stand tolerably nigh the railing, on which I clambered, and with almost unspeakable joy I found myself once more seated on his back. I had another piece of good fortune; for, before I had gone far, a neighbour happened to be passing, who, seeing a child so circumstanced, came up, asked me some questions, heard the story I had to tell, and not only conveyed me safe to the village, but to his own house, where he gave me something comfortable to eat and drink, sent the horse to its right owner, and put me into the charge of some one, who took me home.*

I know nothing that tends so much as the anecdotes of childhood, when faithfully recorded, to guide the philosopher through that very abstruse but important labyrinth, the gradations that lead to the full stature, peculiar form, temperament, character, and qualities of the man. I am therefore anxious to recount all those concerning myself, which I suppose may conduce to this purpose.

* Mr. Holcroft has made use of this incident in the first Volume of Hugh Trevor, see p. 40.

My father was very fond, and not a little vain, of me. He delighted to shew how much I was superior to other children, and this propensity had sometimes a good effect. One evening when it was quite dark, day-light having entirely disappeared, and the night being cloudy, he was boasting to a neighbour of my courage; and his companion seeming rather to doubt, my father replied, he would put it immediately to the proof. "Tom," said he, "you must go to the house of Farmer such a one," (I well remember the walk, but not the name of the person,) "and ask whether he goes to London to morrow." I was startled, but durst not dispute his authority, it was too great over me, besides that my vanity to prove my valor was not a little excited: accordingly I took my hat, and immediately obeyed.

The house I was sent to, as far as I can remember, must have been between a quarter and half a mile distant; and the road that led to it, was by the side of the hedge on the left hand of the Common. However, I knew the way well enough, and proceeded; but it was with many stops, starts, and fears. It may be proper to observe here, that although I could not have been without courage, yet I was really, when a child, exceedingly apprehensive, and full of superstition. When I saw magpies, it denoted good or ill luck, according as they did or did not cross me. When walking, I pored for pins, or rusty nails; which, if they lay in certain directions, foreboded some misfortune. Many such whims possessed my brain—I was therefore not at all free from notions of this kind, on the present occasion. However, I went forward on my errand, humming, whistling, and looking as carefully as I could; now and then making a false step, which helped to relieve me, for it obliged me to attend to the road. When I came to the farm-house, I delivered my message. "Bless me, child," cried the people within, "have you come, this dark night, all alone?" "Oh yes," I said, assuming an air of self-consequence. "And who sent you?" "My father wanted to *know*," I replied equivocally. One of them then offered to take me home, but of this I would by no means admit. My whole little stock of vanity was roused, and I hastily scampered out of the house, and was hidden in the dark. My return was something, but not much less alarming than my journey thither. At last I got safely home, glad to be rid of my fears, and inwardly not a little elated with my success. "Did you hear or see any body,

Tom," said my father, "as you went or came back?" "No," said I, "it was quite dark; not but I thought once or twice, I did hear something behind me." In fact, it was my father and his companion, who had followed me at a little distance. This, my father, in fondly praising me for my courage, some time after told me.

CHAP. III.

"ALL that I now recollect more of this residence in Berkshire is, that my father, after having been from home longer than usual, put a sudden, and to me unexpected end to it—took me with him, and for some time travelled round the country.

The first place I distinctly remember myself, was London, where I have a faint notion of having been among boys with their school-books. Whether I was sent to school for a week or two, while my father and mother were adjusting their affairs, and preparing for their new career, is more than I can affirm or deny: though I have no recollection of acquiring any knowledge, a thing which, before this, had begun to make a strong impression on me. If I were really sent to school, it must have been for a very short time, nor could I have been provided with books or other means of improvement. And indeed my father was so straitened in his circumstances, that my mother very soon after agreed to turn pedlar, hung a basket with pins, needles, tape, garters, and other small haberdashery, on her arm, and hawked them through the outskirts and neighbourhood of London, while I trotted after her. I might at first perhaps feel some disgust at this employment: but use soon reconciled me to it, as the following anecdote will shew.

I cannot say what my father's employment was, while I and my mother were, what they emphatically called *tramping* the villages, to hawk our pedlary. It may be presumed, however that it was not very lucrative, for he soon after left it, and he and my mother went into the country, hawking their small wares, and dragging me after them. They went first to Cambridge, and afterwards, as their hopes of success led them, traversed the neighbouring villages. Among these we came to one which I thought most remarkably clean, well built, and unlike villages in general: my father said it was the handsomest in the kingdom. We must have been very poor, however, and hard-driven on this occasion;

for here it was that I was either encouraged, or commanded, one day to go by myself, from house to house, and beg. Young as I was, I had considerable readiness in making out a story, and on this day, my little inventive faculties shone forth with much brilliancy. I told one story at one house, another at another, and continued to vary my tale just as the suggestions arose: the consequence of which was, that I moved the good country people exceedingly. One called me a poor fatherless child: another exclaimed, what a pity! I had so much sense! a third patted my head, and prayed God to preserve me, that I might make a good man. And most of them contributed either by scraps of meat, farthings, bread and cheese, or other homely offers, to enrich me, and send me away with my pockets loaded. I joyfully brought as much of my stores as I could carry, to the place of rendezvous my parents had appointed, where I astonished them by again reciting the false tales I had so readily invented. My father, whose passions were easily moved, felt no little conflict of mind as I proceeded. I can now, in imagination, see the working of his features. "God bless the boy! I never heard the like!" Then turning to my mother, he exclaimed with great earnestness—"This must not be! the poor child will become a common place liar! A hedge-side rogue!—He will learn to pilfer!—Turn a confirmed vagrant!—Go on the high way when he is older, and get hanged. He shall never go on such errands again." How fortunate for me in this respect, that I had such a father! He was driven by extreme poverty, restless anxiety, and a brain too prone to sanguine expectation, into many absurdities, which were but the harbingers of fresh misfortunes: but he had as much integrity and honesty of heart as perhaps any man in the kingdom, who had had no greater advantages. It pleases me now to recollect, that, though I had a consciousness that my talents could keep my parents from want, I had a still stronger sense of the justice of my father's remarks. As it happened, I had not only read and remembered the consequences of good and evil, as they are pointed out in the Scriptures, but I had also become acquainted with some of the renowned heroes of fable; and to be a liar, a rogue, and get hanged, did not square well with the confused ideas I had either of goodness or greatness, or with my notions of a hero.

From the vicinity of Cambridge, we passed on to the Isle of Ely, hawking our different wares, pins, laces, tempting ribbons, and garters, in every village we came to; arriving first at Peterborough, and afterwards taking care to be present at Wisbeach fair. Markets, fairs, and wakes, were indeed the great objects which regulated all our motions.

The Isle of Ely, from its marshy nature, is much infested by the reptile tribes. One day, as we were pushing forward through the grass by the road side, I saw what I imagined to be a beautiful ribbon, striped and spotted with various colours, but chiefly blue and white; and with great surprise catching hold of my mother's arm, I cried, "Look, mammy, look!" No less admiring what she saw than myself, and equally mistaken,—"Bless me," said she, "how pretty!" Then stooping to take it up, she touched it; but our surprise now greatly increased, when a large snake uncoiled itself, darted forward, and in a moment was out of sight. My father was much amused at the terror we felt. He had lived for some time with a farmer, and knew the difference between the adder and common snake tribes, with the harmless nature of the latter. For in summer and autumn, whenever he could come upon a sleeping snake, he made it his diversion to catch it by the tail, shake it when it attempted to rise, and bring it with him wherever he was going. A country woman, with whom we met shortly after, told us that the breed of snakes was so common in those parts, that they could not be kept out of their cottages, where they frequently took shelter, especially in the night.

The things of which I have the most distinct recollection as connected with the Isle of Ely, are its marshy lands, multiplied ditches, long broad grass, low and numerous draining mills; with the cathedral of Peterborough, which I thought beautiful: but above all, those then dear and delightful creatures, a quack doctor, peeping from behind his curtain, and that droll devil his merry Andrew, apparitions first beheld by me at Wisbeach fair. It was a pleasure so unexpected, so exquisite, so rich and rare, that I followed the merry Andrew and his drummer through the streets, gliding under arms and between legs, never long together three yards apart from him; almost bursting with laughter at his extreme comicality; tracing the gridirons, punchinellos, and pantomime figures on his jacket; wondering at the manner in which he twirled his hat in the air, and again caught it so dexterously on his head. My curiosity did not abate, when he examined to see if there was not some little devil hid within it, with a grotesque squint of his eyes, twist of his nose, and the exclamation, "Oh, ho! have I caught you, Mr. Imp?"—making a snatch at the inside of his hat, grasping at something, opening his hand, finding nothing in it, and then crying with a stupid stare—"No, you see, good folks, the devil of any devil is here!" Then again, when he returned to the stage, followed by an eager crowd, and in an imperious tone was ordered by his master to mount,—to see the comical jump he gave, alighting half upright, roaring with pretended pain, pressing his hip, declaring he had put out his collar bone, crying to his master to come and cure it, receiving a kick, springing up and making a somerset; thanking his master kindly for making him well; yet, the moment his back was turned, mocking him with wry faces; answering the doctor, whom I should have thought extremely witty, if Andrew had not been there, with jokes so apposite and whimsical as never failed to produce roars of laughter. All this was to me assuredly, "the feast of reason and the flow of soul!" As it was the first scene of the kind I had ever witnessed, so it was the most extatic. I think it by no means improbable, that an ardent love of the dramatic art took root in my mind from the accidents of that day.

CHAP. IV.

"THERE are short periods of my life, during which, when endeavouring to retrace them, I am surprised to find I can scarcely recollect any thing of what happened, and this was one of them. How we got from the Isle of

Ely,—where we went,—what we did,—the reasons that induced my father and mother to forsake the business of pedlars,—whether he returned to London for a short time, and again sat down to what he called his trade, namely, that of making, or rather mending shoes,—are questions which I cannot answer. This interval, though not very long, must have been of some duration; for the first remarkable fact that presents itself to my mind, is the strong recollection I have of being at Coventry, walking with my little sister in my arms in a large desolate back yard, at the outskirts of the city. Through this yard, a deep open common sewer ran, into which my sister either sprang, or fell by accident, where she must almost instantly have been suffocated, had not I, instead of being terrified, and running to call for help, immediately thrown myself on the ground, and dragged her safely out. I ran, at once terrified and rejoiced, to tell my father and mother what had happened, and was rewarded by the praises I received from them for the good sense and intrepidity I had shewn. It has been my good fortune to have saved more lives than one, but this was the first.

In and of Coventry itself, I remember several little traits and incidents. I was much taken with the virtue, beauty, and magnanimity of Lady Godina:—the misfortune that befel peeping Tom, was a fine mark of divine justice; and I was equally delighted to think that all the people had bread enough, as I supposed, when the oppressive toll was taken off. Coventry Cross was then standing, and though greatly dilapidated, made no little impression on my imagination, as I walked round and round it, and gazed at its spiral forms, commensurate proportions, numerous little recesses and figures, though half destroyed, that suggested ideas of beauty, sanctity, and the events of past times. Not that I would have it supposed that these ideas passed individually and distinctly through the mind of an uninstructed boy, little more than eight years old, but the effect of them altogether was such as I have here described.

My father, though active and of a strong constitution, was short, slight-built, and wholly unable to contend with men in general. But he was passionate, and free-spoken if he thought himself ill-used, and had thus given offence to a powerful, brutal rival in the market, by whom he was treated with great contempt, and threatened with personal chastisement. I well remember the grief and indignation I then felt that my father should be thus degraded; and that he, I, and all belonging to him, should be unable to redress his wrongs.

This happened on a market-day; and I believe it was on the same day that my father, thinking me almost perished with the cold, gave me a pint of ale to drink, which so far inebriated me, that I was quite ashamed. My father himself was a man of such sobriety, that I had heard him often declare that he had never in his life been overcome with liquor. Besides, I loved religious books, and they all informed me, drunkenness was a great sin. I therefore took it very much to heart that I should so early have been guilty of a crime, of which he was entirely innocent. However, he consoled me by taking the blame upon himself for giving me more to drink than I could be supposed able to bear.

It was here that I saw a person of a

very odd and almost unaccountable appearance. I could not discover whether he was young or old; for he seemed to be both. The size of his limbs, the form of his body, the colour of his hair and face, were such as might have belonged to a boy of eighteen; and to correspond with these he had something of sprightliness in his manner: but his gait and deportment were those of old age: he stooped in the shoulders, and he had the greatest number of small wrinkles in his face that I have ever seen. The reason why I mention many of these (in themselves perhaps insignificant) circumstances, is, that the inquiring reader may be able to trace the bent and progress of my mind, and how far I was prone to observation.

CHAP. V.

" HAVING been bred to an employment for which he was very ill-fitted, both from his physical and mental powers and propensities, the habit that became most rooted in, and most fatal to my father, was a fickleness of disposition, a thorough persuasion, after he had tried one means of providing for himself and family for a certain time, that he had discovered another far more profitable and secure. Steadiness of pursuit was a virtue at which he could never arrive: and I believe few men in the kingdom had in the course of their lives been the hucksters of so many small wares; or more enterprising dealers in articles of a halfpenny value.

Different circumstances have fixed in my mind the recollection of many of the towns to which we went, and a variety of the articles of my father's traffic, but in all probability not a tenth part of either. I at this moment remember in particular, a market-day at Macclesfield in Cheshire; not so much from what we sold, though I believe it was some sort of wooden-ware, of which trenchers and spoons were in those days staple articles, as from a person that caught my attention there. This was a most robust and boisterous woman, more than middle-aged, with a very visible beard, and a deep base voice. I was never weary of listening to, looking at her, and watching all she said or did. I could scarcely think it possible there was such a woman.

I should mention, that to carry on these itinerant trades, my father had begun with purchasing an ass, and bought more as he could; now and then increasing his store by the addition of a ragged poney, or a worn-out, weather-beaten Rozinante. In autumn he turned his attention to fruit, and conveyed apples and pears in hampers from villages to market-towns; among the latter of which I remember, were Tamworth, Newark-upon-Trent, and Hinckley. The bad nourishment I met with, the cold and wretched manner in which I was clothed, and the excessive weariness I endured in following these animals day after day, and being obliged to drive creatures perhaps still more weary than myself, were miseries much too great, and loaded my little heart with sorrows far too pungent ever to be forgotten. Bye roads and high roads were alike to be traversed, but the former far the oftenest, for they were then almost innumerable, and the state of them in winter would scarcely at present be believed.—Speaking of scantiness of diet, an incident happened to me which shews the great power of taste, or rather of imagination, over the appetite, and which ought to be treasured in the memory of those who endeavour to force the appetites of children. I was travelling after my father in Staffordshire near Wosely bridge, where a country-gentleman had a seat. I went into the house, whether alone or for what purpose I totally forget: but I well remember the fragrant steams of the kitchen, and the longing wishes they excited. As I was going away, a good-natured servant said, "Perhaps you are hungry, little boy?" To which, bashfully hanging my head, I answered, "Yes." "Well, then, stop a minute, I'll give you something very nice:" and accordingly, a large bason of rich pease-soup was brought me, and a spoon. I had never eaten, nor perhaps heard of such a thing before: but the moment I smelt it, and applied it to my palate, I conceived such an excessive dislike to it, that though I felt ashamed, and made every effort I could, I found it impossible to swallow a spoonful. Some servants were by my side, and one of them asked, "What! don't you like it? Can't you eat it?" To which, perfectly abashed, and again hanging my head, I replied, "No." "Ha!" said one of them, "you are a dainty chap, however, I wonder who keeps you, or what it is you do like!" I made no reply, but, hungry as I was, and wretchedly disappointed, hurried away as fast as I could, to overtake my father. I should remark, that since I have grown up, pease-soup has always been a favourite dish with me: perhaps, accustomed as I had been from childhood to the plainest food, and empty as my stomach then was, this high-flavoured composition would unavoidably excite disgust.

My father became by turns, a collector and vender of rags, a hardwareman, a dealer in buckles, buttons, and pewter-spoons; in short, a trafficker in whatever could bring gain. But there was one thing which fixed his attention longer than any other, and which therefore, I suppose he found the most lucrative; which was, to fetch pottery from the neighbourhood of Stone, in Staffordshire, and to hawk it through all the North of England. Of all other travelling, this was the most continual, the most severe, and the most intolerable. Derbyshire, Cheshire, Leicestershire, Nottinghamshire, Warwickshire, the towns and cities of Birmingham, Walsall, Wolverhampton, Coventry, Derby, Burton-upon-Trent, Litchfield, Tamworth, Atherstone, Nuneaton, Lutterworth, Ashby-de-la-Zouch, nay, as far up as Warwick, Stratford-upon-Avon, Daventry, Northampton, Newport-Pagnell, Banbury, (I well remember its delicious cakes); and on the east, Stamford in Lincolnshire, Grantham, and in short every place within possible reach, or where pottery might be sold, received visits from my father, the asses, and poor me.

What became of my mother during these excursions, I do not accurately recollect, except that she was with us occasionally, as at Macclesfield for instance, where the woman with the beard and base voice so fixed my attention. She was also with us at Litchfield and Coventry. Most probably she was in general left at home, with her child or children.

By home, I mean an old house half in ruins, about two miles on the north-east side of Rugeley, with a kitchen-garden, paddock, and croft, which afforded some scanty supplies to man and beast, when my father found it convenient, or thought proper to rest a little from his labours; but to me this house often became a den of misery. I was not yet nine years old, but I had a variety of employments. First, I was the messenger of the family to Rugeley, whither I took money, and brought back delicious white bread, for which it was then famous, with such minor articles as were wanted. But when trusted by myself, I could not help loitering on the road, diverting myself with whatever caught my attention, and examining every new object with an idle, boyish curiosity, from which I derived little profit. So that a journey, which ought to have been performed in less than two hours, generally took me more than half a day. I knew the consequences, and had a kind of horror of them, yet could not resist, could not prevail upon myself to go strait forward; such was the united force of habit and curiosity.

My father was alike extreme in his anger, and in his compassion. He used to beat me, pull my hair up by the roots, and drag me by the ears along the ground, till they ran with blood. Indeed my repeated faults were so unpardonable, that he could scarcely blame himself. Yet probably within an hour after he had exercised his severity upon me, he would break out into passionate exclamations of fondness, alarming himself lest he should some time or other do me a serious mischief, and declaring that rather than so, he would a thousand times prefer instant death.

Chastisements like these were grievous, but they were by no means the whole of what I had to encounter. I know not how it happened, but at this early age I was entrusted with business rather like an adult than a child.

Towards Litchfield, on the right, lay Cannock heath and town; and adjoining to this heath, on the left, there were coal-pits situated in a remarkably heavy clay country: (I speak from childish recollection, and may therefore expect to be pardoned, should I in description commit any local errors; as I have never been at Cannock, the coal pits, or the heath, since that period). Desirous of employing his asses, yet averse to go himself (I know not for what reason) my father frequently sent me to these coal-pits to get a single ass loaded, and to drive him over the heath to Rugeley, there to find a customer for my coals. The article was so cheap, and so near, that the profits could be but very small, yet they were something. Had the weather been fine when I was sent on these errands, the task would not have been so difficult, nor the wonder so great; but at the time I was unfortunately sent there, I have a perfect recollection of deep ruts, of cattle, both asses and horses, unable to drag their legs through the clay, and of carts and waggons that were set fast in it. I do not mean that these accidents happened every day, but they were common to the place: and to poor helpless me, with a creature that could scarcely stand under its burthen, they were not less frequent than to others. When any body that could assist me happened to be near, I thought myself in luck; but if I was obliged to run from coal-pit to coal-pit, to request the man who turned the wheel to come and help me, the chance of compliance was little. I often got nothing but a surly curse and a denial; so till some unlooked-for accident brought me relief, there my loaded ass, sometimes heaving a groan at what he suffered, was obliged to stay.

The most remarkable instance of this kind of distress may perhaps deserve recounting. One day, my ass had passed safely through the clay ruts and deep roads, and under my guidance had begun to ascend a hill we had to cross on Cannock heath on our way to Rugeley. The wind was very high; though while we were on low ground, I had never suspected its real force. But my apprehensions began to increase with our ascent, and when on the summit of the hill, nearly opposite to two clumps of trees, which are pictured to my imagination as they stood there at that time, it blew gust after gust, too powerful for the loaded animal to resist, and down it came. Through life I have always had a strong sense of the grief and utter despair I then felt. But what a little surprises me is, that I have no recollection whatever of the means by which I found relief, but rather of the naked and desolate place in which I was, and my inability to help myself. Could I have unloaded the ass, it would not have been much matter; but the coals were brought from the pits in such masses, that three of them were generally an ass-load; any one of which was usually beyond my strength. I have no doubt, however, but I got them by some means or other to Rugeley, and brought the money for them safe to my father, whom I could not help secretly accusing of insensibility, though that was the very reverse of his character.

The coal-pits were situated on the extremity of an old forest, inhabited by large quantities of red deer. At these I always stopped to look: but what surprised and delighted me most was the noble stag; for to him the deer appeared insignificant. Him I often saw bounding along, eying objects without fear, and making prodigious leaps over obstacles that opposed his passage. In this free state, indeed, he cannot but excite our admiration.

One little anecdote I must not omit. The reader will naturally suppose that from the time I began to travel the country with my father and mother, I had little leisure or opportunity to acquire any knowledge by reading. I was too much pressed by fatigue, hunger, cold, and nakedness. Still however I cannot but suppose, as well from my own propensity to obey the will of God, as from my father's wish to encourage my inclinations of this kind, that I continued to repeat my prayers and catechism morning and evening, and on Sundays to read the prayer-book and bible. At any rate, I had not forgot to read; for while we were at the house near Rugeley, by some means or other, the song of Chevy Chace came into my possession, which I read over with great delight at our fire-side. My father, who knew that my memory was tolerably retentive, and saw the great number of stanzas the ballad contained, said to me, "Well, Tom, can you get that song by heart?" To this question I very readily answered, "yes." "In how long a time?"— "Why, you know, father, I have got such work for to-morrow, and what work you will set me for the following days, I can't tell; however, I can get it in three days." "What, perfectly?" "Yes." "Well, if you do that, I'll give you a halfpenny." Rejoiced at my father's generosity, "Oh then, never fear," said I. I scarcely need add, that my task was easily accomplished, and that I then had the valuable sum of a halfpenny at my own disposal.

CHAP. VI.

"THERE was a single instance in which I travelled on foot thirty miles in one day. Whether the miles were measured or computed, is a circumstance which I now forget: but the roads were so heavy, owing to a strong clay soil, that the last quarter of a mile I had to go, I was obliged to confess I could walk no farther, and I was carried on a countryman's shoulders. All those who heard of this, and knew how young, how slight of limb, and stunted in my growth I was, expressed their astonishment, and some their doubts. I think this happened before I was ten years of age.

My father broke up his little establishment near Rugeley, and took me with him into Cheshire, but left me at a village two or three miles from Haslem, where I was intrusted to the care of an old woman, who kept a lodging-house; and whom from the whole of her appearance, as well as her kindness to me, I always remembered with respect. On the evening of my arrival, but later, two travelling Irishmen came in, and were admitted as lodgers. My father had bargained with the old woman, that she was to provide for me: travellers, of course, who come in at sun-set, and depart at day-break, provide for themselves, or are obliged to be satisfied with what such barren abodes can supply. The Irishmen had provided a halfpenny roll between them; what they might have more I do not know. But my good old dame they noticed to be mashing up a plentiful supper of new milk and potatoes for me, a dish in which their hearts delighted. Whether it was contrivance, accident, or according to rule, I cannot say; we did not, however, sup in the presence of the old woman, but in the room in which we all three slept. No sooner were we here, and I had begun in imagination to devour my delicate mashed potatoes, than the Irishmen came up to me, patted my cheeks, told me what a pretty little boy I was, asked me my name, inquired who took care of me, and to what country I was going; and swore by the holy father they never in all their lives, saw so sweet a looking boy, and so compliant and good-tempered. "Do now," said one of them, "let me taste of your mashed potatoes." "Aye, and me too," said the other—"I *warrand* you don't much care about them! We now are a *dale* more used to them in Ireland: I'm sure you'll be very glad to make an exchange. Here now, here is a very fine half-penny roll, which is very nice *ating*, and which to be sure we bought for our own supper. To be sure, we should be fond enough of it, but we don't care about trifles; and as we have been used to *ate* potatoes all the days of our lives, and you English all like bread, why if you *plase*, my sweet compliable *fillow*, we will just make a little bit of a swap, and so we shall all *ate* our suppers heartily." The action followed the word; they took my potatoes, and gave me the dry roll: while I, totally disconcerted, and not a little overawed by the wildness of my fellow-lodgers' looks, the strangeness of their brogue, their red whiskers, dark beards, carotty wigs, and sparkling black eyes, said not a word, but quietly submitted, though I thoroughly regretted the dainty supper I had lost, and saw them devour it with an aching heart.

Whenever I write dialogues like these, it is not to be supposed that I pretend to repeat word for word what was said: after the lapse of so many years, such a pretension would on the face of it be absurd. But I do on all such occasions pretend to give a true picture of the impressions that still remain on my mind, to express the tone and spirit in which the words were spoken, and in general to repeat a part of the words themselves.—I cannot too seriously declare that I write these memoirs with a conscious desire to say nothing but the pure truth, the chief intention of them being to excite an ardent emulation in the breasts of youthful readers; by shewing them how difficulties may be endured, how they may be overcome, and how they may at last contribute, as a school of instruction, to bring forth hidden talent.

CHAP. VII.

"NEXT morning early the Irishmen pursued their journey; and when my father returned, I told him in the hearing of our well-meaning old hostess how I had been tricked out of my supper. They immediately joined in reviling the whole Irish nation, concluding as "the great vulgar and the small" generally do on such occasions, that these two fellows, with the cunning kind of robbery they had committed, exhibited a faithful picture of Ireland and Irishmen. 'Till corrected either by great experience, or conscientious inquiry, the human mind has an almost invincible propensity, when any vice which most excites disgust or contempt is remarked in an individual of a particular country, to affirm that it could belong to no one else, and to ascribe it as a general characteristic to the nation at large.

I believe that my father's intentions, when we left Cheshire, were to seclude himself for a time, by working at the shoe-making business; and that for this purpose he took a circuitous route, with a determination to settle at whatever market-town he should find there was a probability of getting employment. This pursuit led us to Northwich, Knutsford, Congleton, Macclesfield, Sheffield, Chappel in le Frith, in which country the scenery astonished me, and where I was particularly struck with three conic barren rocks, which, I remarked to my father, were like three sugar-loaves. We also went to Buxton, Bakewell, Chesterfield, and Mansfield, where sickness detained us for a time. This sickness was a mutual and dangerous fever, which we caught, either by our being unable to reach a lodging-house, or to pay for a lodging, and by our sleeping, in consequence, under a damp hedge, an imprudence that had nearly proved fatal to us; nor have I ever ceased at intervals to feel its effects. Some time after our recovery from the fever, I was seized by an asthma, which became so violent, that it was only occasionally I dared venture from the house. I can give no account how we were maintained, while we were at Mansfield, nor of the means by which we recovered; but I have a perfect picture before me, of a decent, cleanly house, good attendance, and countenances that were kind and cheerful. At the same time, I have no recollection of conceiving ourselves indebted to charity, or of being under any apprehensions of future want; so that I can hardly suppose that the circumstance which first occasioned our illness, arose from pecuniary distress.

After we had recovered sufficient strength, our next remove was to Nottingham, where we lodged in a house not far from the Park, with the Castle in view, and the brook that winds along the low grounds beneath the height on which it is built. A game which I do not remember to have seen played any where else, and which afforded me no little pleasure, was that of two men having each a round bright ball of iron or steel, to which they had the art of giving an elastic right-line direction along the pathway through the Park; and which, if I am not mistaken, they called playing at long bowls, he who could first attain the goal being the winner. Spell and null, bandy, prison-bars, and other field games, in the address or the activity of which my little heart delighted, long before I was permitted to be a partaker in them, were here among the diversions of the summer evening.

In many parts, Nottingham is, as I then thought it, a very fine town. To me, who had seen so many, its market-place seemed to claim an undoubted and high superiority. Situated on a gently rising ground, that soon becomes dry after showers, surrounded by inns, shops, and other buildings, and well supplied with almost every article, it is among the largest, most convenient, and handsomest in England. A little beyond it were two remarkable inns, the White Lion, and the Blackamoor's Head; each possessed of vast cellarage, wines of I know not what age, with viands, beds, and other conveniences, such as it gave me the greatest satisfaction to hear described.

One of our four principal rivers, the noble Trent, flows through the meadows below the town, at no very great distance. The scenery round it, to my boyish apprehension, was grand. When the day and the stream were clear, I have often taken a particular pleasure in watching the shoals of fish of the smaller kind in which it abounded, or in now and then catching a glimpse of some of greater magnitude, or in seeing them brought on shore by the dexterous angler. A village, called the Hermitage, lay on its banks, and thither I delighted to walk, because it was connected with circumstances, which interested my imagination.— Here, as well as in other places in the outskirts of the town, there were houses cut in the rock; and I could not but fancy them to have been formerly inhabited by a venerable and holy brotherhood of Hermits. These houses were indeed to me objects of the greatest curiosity. I could never cease admiring that men should persevere in hewing themselves out such habitations, and that they should turn a thing so barren to so much use and profit; for these rocks were in fact high banks of sand-stone, and on the top of them, that is, on the roofs of their houses, each man had his garden.

I walked much about at Nottingham in company with my father, to whom I was very eager to communicate all my juvenile pleasures, and of whom I also made constant inquiries with respect to the objects we saw. He, however, could oftener make conjectures than give information. I imagine his reason for taking me thus into the air, was, as he hoped, to arrest the progress of the asthma which daily increased, and became alarming; for there were times when I could not walk above a few yards without standing still to recover breath. Such medical people as my father could obtain access to, were consulted; but the general opinion was that unless youth and growth should relieve me, the disease was for life. An intelligent surgeon happened to think otherwise: he entertained hopes, he said, provided an issue was made, and carefully kept open on the inside of each leg below the knee. My father accepted his offer to perforate the skin, and direct me in dressing the issues; for to my known prudence this care was readily committed. The success of the remedy equalled the expectations of the surgeon. The cure, aided no doubt by my youth and cheerful temperament, was progressively visible from week to week, and my joy and thankfulness to my medical guide were great. Whoever he was, I certainly owe him much; but I have forgotten his name. This must have happened in the year 1756 or 7, but I believe the latter.

CHAP. VIII.

PUBLIC sights, even though cruel, have been, through all ages, the delight of the herd of mankind. The sessions were just over, and a malefactor, who had been sentenced to death, was left by the judge for execution. My father proposed that we should accompany the crowd, and see what was to be seen. To this I consented; we followed the cart to the gallows which stood at some distance from the town; and by talking with each other, listening to remarks that were made, some of them charitable, others tainted with a revengeful spirit, and by frequently stopping to observe the agitation of the poor wretch whose life was so soon to cease, I was thrown into a very pensive state of mind. However, taking my father by the hand, I patiently waited the awful moment when the cap was drawn over the culprit's eyes, and he was suddenly lifted into the air. Here his convulsive struggles, to my young and apprehensive imagination, were intolerable: I soon turned my eyes away, unable to look any longer; and my father seeing the pain I was in, said, "Come, Tom, let us go." "Oh yes, yes, father, as fast as we can," was my reply. The effect on my mind was such, that I made, as I suppose, the first fixed resolution of my life, and declared it in a tone that denoted how determined I was,—"Never again, while I live," said I, "will I go, and see a malefactor put to death." Five or six and twenty years afterwards, I thought it an act of duty to change this determination when I was first at Paris in the year 1783. Through life, however, when hanging, and the various ways in which men exterminate each other, have been talked of, I have rarely, if ever, forgotten the poor dying culprit of Nottingham.

It should seem that men have at all times had the good sense to contrast their melancholy and often disgusting institutions, with others of an opposite tendency; and that seldom fail in the very nature of them to revive the sickening heart, and give it animation and delight.

The time of Nottingham Races drew near. My father was a great lover of horses, as I have said; and from his discourse, as well as the little I had seen of these noble animals, I was eager to become better acquainted with them. My father recapitulated the different places at which he had seen horses run, recounted the names of the famous winners he had known, and filled up the picture with the accidents common on such occasions, the amazing cunning of sharpers, the punishments inflicted on some of their detected rogueries; the cries of the betting chair, the tumult of the crowd when the horses were running, the danger of being too near the course, with the difficulty of keeping it clear, the multitude of gaming and drinking booths, and all that variety of delightful commotion which was calculated to gratify my boyish fancy. The whole scene was like enchantment; and all my wishes were now centered in its being realised.

Ten days or a fortnight before the time, straggling horses for the different plates began to drop in; and of course to take their morning and evening exercise on the course, where they might be seen. This was a pleasure not to be neglected either by me or my father. I was delighted with the fineness of their limbs, their glossy coats;

and not a little amused, when following them from exercise to the stable, if I were but allowed to take a peep, and see how their body-clothes were managed, how the currying and brushing of them was performed, their high straw beds prepared, their long hay carefully chosen, and their oats sifted and re-sifted. Every thing about a race-horse is precious: but I pitied them for being so much stinted in their food, and especially when my father told me it must daily decrease, and that the night before they started they must fast.

But the great and glorious part which Nottingham held in the annals of racing this year, arose from the prize of the King's plate, which was to be contended for by the two horses which every body I heard speak considered as undoubtedly the best in England, and perhaps equal to any that had ever been known, Childers alone excepted. Their names were, Careless and Atlas. Careless, who had been bred by a worthy and popular Baronet of the county (I forget his name) was the decided favourite of every man in Nottingham, gentle or simple. The prowess and equal, if not superior, merit of Atlas, were very boldly asserted by strangers, and particularly by jockeys, betters, and men of the turf. If I do not mistake, Atlas was the property of, and bred by the Duke of Devonshire. However, he had received a previous defeat in running against Careless; and this defeat the men of Nottingham considered as little less than a certainty of future victory. The opposite party affirmed that Atlas, being a remarkably powerful horse (I think seventeen hands high), had not then attained his full force. There was a story in circulation concerning him, which if true deserved to be remembered. He was a full bred horse out of the Duke's own stud, and consequently was intended for training: but being unwieldy when foaled, and as he grew up becoming still more so, he was rejected on account of his size and clumsiness, and banished to the cart breed. Among these inferiors he remained, till by some accident, either of playfulness or fright, several of them started together, and the vast advantage of Atlas in speed happening to be noticed, it was then thought proper by the grooms to restore him to his blood companions.

Of those who in the least amused or busied themselves with such affairs, Careless and Atlas occupied the whole discourse. Many people who seemed to reason plausibly enough on the subject, affirmed that if any thing lost the race to Careless, it would be the inferior skill of his rider, by whom neither he ground nor the powers of the horse would be well economized; he was nerely the groom of a country gentle- nan. When the race was over, these ccusations were vociferated with wea- isome reiteration.

On the appointed day, however, hey both started for the king's plate; nd I believe there was scarcely a heart n the race-course, that did not swell with hope and fear. As for my own little one, it was all in rapture for Careless. He was so finely made, his coat was so bright, his eye so beaming, his limbs so animated, and every motion seemed so evidently to declare, "I can fly, if I please," that I could not endure the thought of his being conquered. Alas for the men of Nottingham, conquered he was! I forget whether it was at two or three heats, but there was many an empty purse on that night, and many a sorrowful heart.

CHAP. IX.

"THESE different incidents had raised a strong desire in my mind to be better acquainted with a subject that had given to me, and as I thought to every body, so much emotion, and I began to consider what might be done. At that time I was rather a burthen to my father than a help. I believe I assisted him a little in the mending of shoes, but my asthma till very lately, as well as my youth, had prevented my making much progress. At one time indeed I had been persuaded, though much against my will, to become apprentice to a stocking-weaver; but this, I forget how, broke off, at which I was very glad: I did not like stocking-weaving. The question now occurred to me, whether it would not be possible to procure the place of a stable-boy, at Newmarket. I was at this time in point of clothing in a very mean, not to say ragged condition, and in other respects, was not much better off. The stable-boys I saw at Nottingham, were healthy, clean, well fed, well clothed, and remarkable rather for their impudence, than seeming to live under any kind of fear or hardship. Except their impudence, I liked every thing else I saw about them; and concluded that if I could obtain so high a situation as this, I should be very fortunate.

These reflections preyed so much upon my mind, that I was at last induced to mention them to my father; and he having a predilection for every thing belonging to a horse, and therefore a high respect for this, the noblest state of that animal's existence, readily fell into my views, and only feared they could not be accomplished. He resolved however that trial should be made; and after inquiring among the Jockeys, thought it advisable to apply to a Mr. Woodcock, who kept stables four or five miles from Newmarket, where he trained horses entrusted to his care. Mr. Woodcock examined me, asked my age, found I was light of weight, and, as I suppose, liking the answers I gave to his questions, to our very great joy, agreed to take me upon trial. In the course of my life, there have been several changes, that each in their turn, greatly affected my spirits, and gave me advantages far beyond what I had ever before enjoyed: of these gradual elevations, this was the first. I should now be somebody. I should be entrusted with the management of one of that race of creatures that were the most admired and beloved by me: I should be well clothed, wear a livery, which would shew I belonged to one of the great: I should not only have food enough, but of that kind which was highly relishing to the appetite of youth; and, in addition to all this, should receive an annual stipend. I jumped as it were, from a precarious and mean existence, where I could not tell what worse might happen, into a permanent and agreeable employment. I had only to learn to ride, and perform the duties of a stable-boy, of which I had no fear, for I supposed them far less difficult than I afterwards found they were.

The grooms that reside at, and in the vicinity of this famed town, are all more or less, acquainted with each other; and on Mr. Woodcock's recommendation, I was put under the care of Jack Clarke, who lived with Captain Vernon, he having luckily a led horse, which I was to mount. The day of parting with my father, and of beginning our journey, was an anxious one. He could not too emphatically repeat the few well meant precepts he had so often given me, nor I too earnestly assure him, I would love and obey him all my life. Notwithstanding his severity, he was passionately fond of me, my heart entered into the same feelings, and there was great and unfeigned affection between us.

CHAP. X.

"As is the custom in travelling with trained horses, we set off early, and walked without hurry. When we stopped to breakfast, the plenty of excellent cold beef, bread and cheese, with the best table-beer, and as much as we pleased, gave me a foretaste of the fortunate change I had made. This indeed exceeded my utmost expectations,—I was entering upon a new existence,—was delighted, full of hope, and cheerful alacrity, yet too timid to be presumptuous. Clarke, being a good-tempered lad, and seeing me happy, attempted to play me no tricks whatever. On the contrary, he gave me all the caution and advice he could, to guard me against being drawn into the common-place deceptions, most of them nasty, many of them unhealthy, and all of them tending to make the poor tyro, a common laughing-stock, uniformly practised by the resident boys, upon every new comer. I do not recollect one-half these tricks: but that with which they begin, if I do not mistake, is to persuade their victim, that the first thing necessary for a well-trained stable-boy, is to borrow as many waistcoats as he can, and in the morning after he has dressed and fed his horse, to put them all on, take a race of perhaps two or three miles, return home, strip himself stark naked, and immediately be covered up in the hot dung-hill; which, they assure him, is the method the grooms take when they sweat themselves down to ride a race. Should the poor fellow follow their directions, they conclude the joke with pail-fulls of cold water, which stand ready, to throw over him.

Another of their diversions used to be that of hunting the owl, which is already very whimsically described in a book of much humour, and tolerably well-known, called Tim Bobbin's Lancashire dialect. To catch the owl, is to persuade a booby that there is an owl found at roost in the corner of a barn; that a ladder must be placed against a hole, through which, when the persons within shall be pleased to hoot and hunt him, he must necessarily fly, as the barn door is shut, and every other outlet closed: that the boy chosen to catch the owl must mount this ladder on the outside, and the purblind animal, they say, will fly directly into his hat. When the owl-catcher is persuaded to all this, and mounts to his post, the game begins: hallooing and absurd noises are made; the fellows within divert themselves with laughing at what is to come, and pretending to call to one another to drive the owl from this place to that; while two or three of them approach nearer and nearer to the hole, when they discharge the contents of their full tubs and pails on the head of the expecting owl-catcher, who is generally precipitated from his ladder to some soft, but not very agreeable preparation below.

Clarke warned me against several other of the games at which I should be invited to play; in most of which there was some whim, but a great deal more of that dirty wit in which ill-bred boys are known to delight. Clarke, however, did me this essential service, that he not only taught me to avoid all the snares he mentioned, but rendered me so wary, that all the time I was among this mischievous crew, I was never once entrapped by them. At this they occasionally expressed great wonder; perhaps, had they known the secret, they would have taken their revenge on Clarke.

The weather through the whole of our journey was fine, the ride highly agreeable, and the instruction and information I received from Clarke, made it still more pleasant to me. The only place I can distinctly remember having passed through and made a short stay at, was Huntingdon.

CHAP. XI.

"As I have said, Mr. Woodcock resided in the vicinity of Newmarket, at the distance of three or four miles; and to the house where he lived Clarke immediately took me, gave up his charge, and we parted, I believe with mutual good-will: at least, my feelings towards him were grateful and friendly. As a thing of course, there must have been stables belonging to the house of Mr. Woodcock, but I cannot recollect what train he had under him; and to say the truth, I cannot fix upon any one figure, man, boy, or animal, except a grey filly, on the back of which I was put, and which I was entrusted with the care of.

I doubt if Mr. Woodcock was at home on my arrival. His family was small; and had the air of being genteel. It consisted of himself, his wife, and their daughter, who was about eleven years old. All that I can now recollect of Mrs. and Miss Woodcock, is, having seen them very neatly dressed in white, that the mother assumed a very superior but obliging manner, and that I stood much in awe of her. Trees were thinly scattered to some distance round the house: the parlour was very neat, and rather spacious. In this I received one of those early lessons in moral honesty, which produce a greater effect on the mind of a child, or even of a youth, than is generally supposed. One afternoon, the tea-things and sugar-bason being set out in the parlour before Mrs. and Miss Woodcock had come down, I was passing the door, and that delicious bait of boyhood, a fine lump of sugar, caught my eye. I looked, considered, looked again, saw nobody, found it irresistible, and venturing step by step on tiptoe, seized the tempting prize, thinking myself secure: but as I turned back to hasten away with it, the first object that struck me was a young gentleman, stretched either on a chair or sopha behind the door, with a book in his hand, a look directed to me, and a smile on his countenance. I cannot express the shame I felt: but I immediately returned the sugar to its place, cast down my eyes, and slunk away, most heartily mortified, especially when the young gentleman's smile broke out into a laugh.

I forgot to mention, though it will easily be supposed, that when I entered on my new profession, my dress was changed, and I was made to look something like a stable-boy.

Miss Woodcock was a very neat little girl, and it somehow happened, though I know not by what means, that I soon got rather in favour with her. She would whisper with me when we met near the house, chide me if she saw what she thought an impropriety, and once or twice condescended to be half or quite angry with me, while I did all in my power to please her. These trifling advances, however, which spoke rather the innocence of the age, than the intention of the mind, were soon put an end to by an accident that had nearly proved fatal to me.

Perfectly a novice as I was, though I could sit with seeming safety on a quiet horse, I neither knew how to keep a firm seat, nor suddenly to seize one, and I was almost certain of being thrown if any thing that was but a little violent or uncommon happened. I was walking the dark grey filly quite a foot-pace in the forest, when in an instant something startled her, and made her spring aside: by which I was not only unseated and thrown, but unfortunately for me, my foot hung in the stirrup; her fright was increased, she began to kick and plunge violently, and I received a blow in the stomach, which, though it freed me from the stirrup, left me, as was supposed, for no inconsiderable time, dead. Somebody, I imagine, was riding with me, for the alarm was soon given: I was taken up, carried home, treated with great humanity, and by bleeding and other medical means, signs of life at length became visible. All that I myself recollect of a circumstance so very serious, and so very near being mortal, was, that I was thrown, kicked, and dreadfully frightened; that some time afterwards I found myself very ill in bed, in a very neat chamber, and that I was spoken to and attended with great kindness till my recovery.

This accident, however, put an end to my jockeyship in the service of Mr. Woodcock: he discovered a little too late, that the dark grey filly and I could not be trusted safely together. But though he turned me away, he did not desert me. He recommended me to the service of a little deformed groom, remarkably long in the fork, I think of the name of Johnstone, who was esteemed an excellent rider, and had a string of no less than thirteen famous horses, the property of the Duke of Grafton, under his care. This was acknowledged to be a service of great repute: but the shrewd little groom soon discovered that I had all my trade to learn, and I was again dismissed.

After this new disappointment, I felt perhaps a more serious alarm than is usual with boys at such an age. For, independently of natural sensibility, I had seen so much of the world, had so often been intrusted with its petty affairs, depended so much upon my ability to act for myself, and had been so confident in my assurances to my father that I ran no risk in venturing alone into the world, that my fears were not trifling when I found myself so far from him, thrown out of place, and convicted of being unable to perform the task I had so inconsiderately undertaken. Mr. Johnstone told me I must endeavour to get a place, but that for his part he could say little in my favour; however, he would suffer me to remain a few days among the boys. My despondency was the greater, because, the morning before, when a horse that I was riding shook himself in his saddle, as horses are sometimes observed to do, I fell from his back as much terrified as if he had been rearing, plunging, and kicking. To hardy grooms, and boys that delight in playing the braggart, this was a truly ridiculous instance of cowardice, and was repeated with no little malignity and laughter.

CHAP. XII.

"THE unforeseen relief, that has been given to misfortune under circumstances apparently quite hopeless, has frequently been remarked, and not seldom affirmed to be an incontestible proof of a particular providence.

I know not where I got the information, nor how, but in the very height of my distress, I heard that Mr. John Watson, training and riding groom to Captain Vernon, a gentleman of acute notoriety on the turf, and in partnership with the then Lord March, the present Duke of Queensbury, was in want of, but just then found it difficult to procure a stable-boy. To make this pleasing intelligence still more welcome, the general character of John Watson was, that, though he was one of the first grooms in Newmarket, he was remarkable for being good-tempered: yet the manner in which he disciplined his boys, though mild, was effectual, and few were in better repute. One consequence of this, however, was, that, if any lad was dismissed by John Watson, it was not easy for him to find a place.

With him Jack Clarke lived, the lad with whom I came from Nottingham: this was another fortunate circumstance, and contributed to inspire me with confidence. My present hopes were so strongly contrasted with my late fears, that they were indeed enviable. To speak for once in metaphor, I had been as one of those who walk in the shadow of the valley of death: an accidental beam of the sun broke forth, and I had a beatific view of heaven.

It was no difficult matter to meet with John Watson: he was so attentive to stable-hours, that, except on extraordinary occasions, he was always to be found. Being first careful to make myself look as much like a stable-boy as I could, I came at the hour of four (the summer hour for opening the afternoon stables, giving a slight feed of oats, and going out to evening exercise), and ventured to ask if I could see John Watson. The immediate answer was in the affirmative. John Watson came, looked at me with a serious, but good-natured, countenance, and accosted me first with, "Well, my lad, what is your business? I suppose I can guess; you want a place?"—"Yes, Sir."—"Who have you lived with?"—"Mr. Woodcock, on the forest: one of your boys, Jack Clarke, brought me with him from Nottingham." "How came you to leave Mr. Woodcock?"—"I had a sad fall from an iron grey filly, that almost killed me."—"That is bad indeed!—and so you left him?"—"He turned me away, Sir."—"That is honest: I like your speaking the truth. So you are come from him to me?" At this question I cast my eyes down, and hesitated, then fearfully answered, "No, Sir."—"No!

what, change masters twice in so short a time?"—"I can't help it, Sir, if I am turned away." This last answer made him smile. "Where are you now, then?"—"Mr. Johnstone gave me leave to stay with the boys a few days." "That is a good sign. I suppose you mean little Mr. Johnstone at the other end of the town?"—"Yes, Sir."—"Well, as you have been so short a time in the stables, I am not surprised he should turn you away: he would have every body about him as clever as himself, they must all know their business thoroughly. However they must learn it somewhere. I will venture to give you a trial, but I must first inquire your character of my good friends, Woodcock and Johnstone. Come to-morrow morning at nine, and you shall have an answer."

It may well be supposed I did not forget the appointment; and a fortunate one I found it, for I was accepted on trial at four pounds or guineas a year, with the usual livery clothing. My station was immediately assigned me. Here was a remarkably quiet three years old colt, lately from the discipline of the breaker; and of him I was ordered to take charge, instructed by one of the upper boys in every thing that was to be done, and directed to back him and keep pace with the rest, when they went to exercise, only taking care to keep a strait line, and to walk, canter, and gallop the last. Fortunately for me his temper appeared to be so quiet (for he had been put into full training at an early age), that I found not the least difficulty in managing him. My reputation, therefore, among the boys, which is an essential circumstance, suffered no stain.

I ought to mention, that though I have spoken of Mr. Johnstone, and may do of more Misters among the grooms, it is only because I have forgotten their christian names: for, to the best of my recollection, when I was at Newmarket, it was the invariable practice to denominate each groom by his christian and surname, unless any one happened to possess some peculiarity that marked him. For instance, I remember a little man in years, grown timid from age, but otherwise supposed to be the best rider in England, and remarkable for his knowledge of almost every race-course, whose name, I think, was William Cheevers; and of whom it was the custom to speak, by calling him Old Will, The Old One, and the like. I mention this, as it may be now or hereafter, a distinctive mark of the changes of manners. I know not what appellations are given to grooms at Newmarket at the present day, but at the time I speak of, if any grooms had been called Misters, my master would certainly have been among the number; and his constant appellation by every body, except his own boys who called him John, was simply John Watson.

With respect to me, his conduct seems to shew that he understood my character better than the grooms who had judged of it before: as I did not long ride a quiet colt at the tail of the string (on whose back he soon put a new-comer), but had a dun horse, by no means a tame or safe one, committed to my care. Instead of timidity, he must have remarked various traits of courage in me, before he would have ventured on this step. In corroboration of this I may cite the following proof. I continued to ride the dun horse through the winter. It was John Watson's general practice to exercise his horses over the flat, and up Cambridge hill on the west side of Newmarket;

but the rule was not invariable. One wintry day he ordered us up to the Bury hills. It mizzled a very sharp sleet, the wind became uncommonly cutting, and Dun, the horse I rode, being remarkable for a tender skin, found the wind and the sleet, which blew directly up his nostrils, so very painful, that it suddenly made him outrageous. He started from the rank in which he was walking, tried to unseat me, endeavoured to set off full speed, and when he found he could not master me so as to get head, began to rear, snorted most violently, threw out behind, plunged, and used every mischievous exertion, of which the muscular powers of a blood horse are capable. I, who felt the uneasiness he suffered before his violence began, being luckily prepared, sat firm, as steady and upright, as if this had been his usual exercise. John Watson was riding beside his horses, and a groom, I believe it was old Cheevers, broke out into an exclamation—"By God, John, that is a fine lad!" "Aye, aye," replied Watson, highly satisfied, "you will find some time or other there are few in Newmarket that will match him." To have behaved with true courage, and to meet with applause like this, especially from John Watson, was a triumph, such as I could at this time have felt in no other way with the same sweet satisfaction. My horsemanship had been seen by all the boys,—my praises had been heard by them all.

It will not be amiss here to remark that boys with strait legs, small calves, and knees that project but little, seldom become excellent riders. I, on the contrary, was somewhat bow-legged, I had then the custom of turning in my toes, and my knees were protuberant. I soon learned that the safe hold for sitting steady was to keep the knee and the calf of the leg strongly pressed against the side of the animal that endeavours to unhorse you: and as little accidents afford frequent occasions to remind the boys of this rule, it becomes so rooted in the memory of the intelligent, that their danger is comparatively trifling.

Of the temperaments and habits of blood horses there are great varieties, and those very strongly contrasted. The majority of them are playful, but their gambols are dangerous to the timid or unskilful. They are all easily and suddenly alarmed, when any thing they do not understand forcibly catches their attention, and they are then to be feared by the bad horseman, and carefully guarded against by the good. Very serious accidents have happened to the best. But, besides their general disposition to playfulness, there is a great propensity in them to become what the jockeys call vicious. High-bred, hot in blood, exercised, fed, and dressed so as to bring that heat to perfection, their tender skins at all times subject to a sharp curry-comb, hard brushing, and when they take sweats, to scraping with wooden instruments, it cannot be but that they are frequently and exceedingly irritated. Intending to make themselves felt and feared, they will watch their opportunity to bite, stamp, or kick; I mean those among them that are vicious. Tom, the brother of Jack Clarke, after sweating a grey horse that belonged to Lord March, with whom he lived, while he was either scraping or dressing him, was seized by the animal by the shoulder, lifted from the ground, and carried two or three hundred yards before the horse loosened his hold. Old Forester, a horse that belonged to Captain Vernon all the while I remained at Newmarket, was obliged to be kept apart, and being foundered, to live at grass, where he was confined to a close paddock. Except Tom Watson, a younger brother of John, he would suffer no lad to come near him: if in his paddock, he would run furiously at the first person that approached, and if in the stable, would kick and assault every one within his reach. Horses of this kind seem always to select their favourite boy. Tom Watson, indeed, had attained to man's estate, and in his brother's absence, which was rare, acted as superintendent. Horses, commonly speaking, are of a friendly and generous nature; but there are anecdotes of the malignant and savage ferocity of some, that are scarcely to be credited: at least many such are traditional at Newmarket.

Of their friendly disposition towards

their keepers, there is a trait known to every boy that has the care of any one of them, which ought not to be omitted. The custom is to rise very early, even between two and three in the morning, when the days lengthen. In the course of the day, horses and boys have much to do. About half after eight, perhaps, in the evening, the horse has his last feed of oats, which he generally stands to enjoy in the centre of his smooth, carefully made bed of clean long straw, and by the side of him the weary boy will often lie down: it being held as a maxim, a rule without exception, that were he to lie even till morning, the horse would never lie down himself, but stand still, careful to do his keeper no harm. I should add, however, that the boy must keep awake, not for fear of the horse, but of the mischievous disposition of his comrades. Should sleep happen to overcome him, some lad will take one of those tough ashen plants with which they ride, and measuring his aim, strike him with all his force, and endeavour to make the longest wale he possibly can, on the leg of the sleeper. I remember to have been so punished once, when the blow, I concluded, was given by Tom Watson, as I thought no other boy in the stable could have made so large a wale: it reached from the knee to the instep, and was of a finger's breadth.

CHAP. XIII.

THERE are few trades or professions, each of which has not a uniform mode of life peculiar to it, subject only to such slight variations as are incidental and temporary. This observation is particularly applicable to the life of a stable-boy.

All the boys in the stable rise at the same hour, from half-past two in spring, to between four and five in the depth of winter. The horses hear them when they awaken each other, and neigh, to denote their eagerness to be fed. Being dressed, the boy begins with carefully clearing out the manger, and giving a feed of oats, which he is obliged no less carefully to sift. He then proceeds to dress the litter; that is, to shake the bed on which the horse has been lying, remove whatever is wet or unclean, and keep the remaining straw in the stable for another time. The whole stables are then thoroughly swept, the few places for fresh air are kept open, the great heat of the stable gradually cooled, and the horse, having ended his first feed, is roughly cleaned and dressed. In about half an hour after they begin, or a little better, the horses have been rubbed down, and re-clothed, saddled, each turned in his stall, then bridled, mounted, and the whole string goes out to morning exercise; he that leads being the first: for each boy knows his place.

Except by accident, the race-horse never trots. He must either walk or gallop; and in exercise, even when it is the hardest, the gallop begins slowly and gradually, and increases till the horse is nearly at full speed. When he has galloped half a mile, the boy begins to push him forward, without relaxation, for another half-mile. This is at the period when the horses are in full exercise, to which they come by degrees. The boy that can best regulate these degrees among those of light weight, is generally chosen to lead the gallop; that is, he goes first out of the stable, and first returns.

In the time of long exercise, this is the first *brushing gallop.* A brushing gallop signifies that the horses are nearly at full speed before it is over, and it is commonly made at last rather up hill. Having all pulled up, the horses stand some two or three minutes, and recover their wind; they then leisurely descend the hill and take a long walk; after which they are brought to water. But in this, as in every thing else (at least as soon as long exercise begins), every thing to them is measured. The boy counts the number of times the horse swallows when he drinks, and allows him to take no more gulps than the groom orders, the fewest in the hardest exercise, and one horse more or less than another, according to the judgment of the groom.—After watering, a gentle gallop is taken, and after that, another walk of considerable length; to which succeeds the second and last brushing gallop, which is by far the most severe. When it is over, another pause thoroughly to recover their wind is allowed them, their last walk is begun, the limits of which are prescribed, and it ends in directing their ride homewards.

The morning's exercise often extends to four hours, and the evening's to much about the same time. Being once in the stable, each lad begins his labour. He leads the horse into his stall, ties him up, rubs down his legs with straw, takes off his saddle and body clothes; curries him carefully, then with both curry-comb and brush, never leaves him till he has thoroughly cleaned his skin, so that neither spot nor wet, nor any appearance of neglect may be seen about him. The horse is then reclothed, and suffered to repose for some time, which is first employed in gratifying his hunger, and recovering from his weariness. All this is performed, and the stables are once more shut up, about nine o'clock.

Accustomed to this life, the boys are very little overcome by fatigue, except that early in the morning they may be drowsy. I have sometimes fallen slightly asleep at the beginning of the first brushing gallop. But if they are not weary, they are hungry, and they make themselves ample amends for all they have done. Nothing perhaps can exceed the enjoyment of a stable-boy's breakfast: what then may not be said of mine, who had so long been used to suffer hunger, and so seldom found the means of satisfying it? Our breakfast consisted of new milk, or milk porridge, then the cold meat of the preceding day, most exquisite Gloucester cheese, fine white bread, and concluded with plentiful draughts of table-beer. All this did not overload the stomach, or in the least deprive me of my youthful activity, except that like others I might sometimes take a nap for an hour, after so small a portion of sleep.

For my own part, so total and striking was the change which had taken place in my situation, that I could not but feel it very sensibly. I was more conscious of it than most boys would have been, and therefore not a little satisfied. The former part of my life had most of it been spent in turmoil, and often in singular wretchedness. I had been exposed to every want, every weariness, and every occasion of despondency, except that such poor sufferers become reconciled to, and almost insensible of suffering, and boyhood and beggary are fortunately not prone to despond. Happy had been the meal where I had enough; rich to me was the rag that kept me warm; and heavenly the pillow, no matter what, or how hard, on which I could lay my head to sleep. Now I was warmly clothed, nay, gorgeously, for I was proud of my new livery, and never suspected that there was disgrace in it; I fed voluptuously, not a prince on earth perhaps with half the appetite, and never-failing relish; and instead of being obliged to drag through the dirt after the most sluggish, obstinate, and despised among our animals, I was mounted on the noblest that the earth contains, had him under my care, and was borne by him over hill and dale, far outstripping the wings of the wind. Was not this a change, such as might excite reflection even in the mind of a boy!

Boys, when at full liberty, and thus kept in health and exercise, are eager at play. The games most common at

Newmarket, were fives, spell and null, marbles, chuck-farthing, and spinning tops, at which, as well as marbles and fives, I excelled. Another game called holes, was occasionally played by a few of the boys. This was a game of some little study, and was much delighted in by the shepherd boys and men, who tended their flocks on that vast plain (as then it was) on which Newmarket stood. Three squares were cut in the earth, one within the other, in each side of which were three holes. Each antagonist had nine warriors or bits of stick to combat the opposing nine. What the rules of the game were, I have forgotten; but I believe the most essential of them was, that he was the victor who could imprison his adversary's men, or leave them no further space to move in. If the choice of the move were given, I, and other good players, knew how to win at this game with certainty. Till I discovered the secret, I was greatly devoted to the game.

In order to have fair play allowed me at these different games, I had my little infant labours of Hercules to perform; or, to speak more properly and plainly, to fight my way, and convince all the boys of my own age, I was not to be cowed by them. All boys are wranglers; and out of this propensity the elder boys at Newmarket take pleasure in creating themselves diversion. Jack Clarke, who was about seventeen, was a very good natured, peaceable lad: but all the others in our stable were very assiduous in exciting the little ones to quarrel, and persuading him, who would have wished to remain at peace, to believe he must certainly be a coward. This stigma I was not willing to be loaded with: the consequence was, that battle after battle was fought, first between me and Jack, and then between me and Tom, for two of us were so named. Jack had been a shepherd boy, was older by some months than myself, preceded me as a jockey, was a most inveterate, obstinate, and unfair antagonist, for he would bite, kick, or do any thing to gain the victory, was quite as strong as myself, and excessively hardy. However, he entirely wanted method and presence of mind; and after three or four desperate contests, he was obliged fairly to own he was not my equal. Tom, who came into the service after me, was likewise older, larger-limbed, and had more strength; but my conquest of him was much more easy. He had bones, sinews, and thews, as Shakspeare says, but little heart; he was prevailed on to venture a second combat, but not a third. I had the good fortune also to face and outface those among

Lord March's boys, who lived opposite to us, and with whom we had continual intercourse; so that, though I was but thirteen, I became the acknowledged hero among the boys of both stables, under fifteen years of age. Thus much for the footing on which I stood with my rivals within the first half-year after I came to live with John Watson. It must be remembered, that all the tricks of which Jack Clarke had warned me, had been tried upon me in vain. These things, together with my aptitude at play, soon placed me as the leading boy of the young fry.

From nine o'clock in the morning till four, the whole time is at the boy's own disposal, except that of breakfasting and dining, which he is seldom apt to think ill employed. But in summer, spring, and autumn, the stables are again opened at four, and woe to him who is absent! I never was but once, when unfortunately Captain Vernon himself happened to arrive at Newmarket. I never saw John Watson so angry with me before or afterwards; though even then, after giving me four or five strokes across the shoulders with an ashen plant, he threw it away in disgust, and exclaimed, as he turned from me—" Damn the boy ! On such a day !"

The business to be done in the afternoon is but a repetition, with little or no variety, of that which I have described for the morning, except that they return to stables at seven, or rather earlier, again dress their horses, give them a first feed, go to supper themselves, give a second feed, prepare the horses' beds, pick and prepare the hay with which they sup, and by nine o'clock the stables are once more shut up, containing both horses and boys.

CHAP. XIV.

THE time I remained at Newmarket, was upwards of two years and a half; during which many things occurred worthy of remembrance; and though in their nature dissimilar, yet all tending to have that influence on character, by which, if my poor philosophy holds good, character is progressively formed. Instead of relating these different accidents as they occurred, I shall rather endeavour to collect them into classes, beginning with those that immediately belong to the business of a jockey.

I have already remarked how necessary it is for the best horseman never to be off his guard. At the time the little accident I am going to relate happened, and which I could not but then consider as rather disgraceful, I was so persuaded of being always on the alert, and of my power of instantaneously recovering my seat, that I supposed what followed to be nearly an impossibility.—The horse that I then rode happened to be unwell; and did not take his morning and evening exercise with the others. I was therefore ordered to walk him out a couple of hours in the middle of the day, to canter him gently, give him a certain quantity of water, and canter and walk him home again. The horse was by no means apt to start or play tricks of an uncommon kind: he was besides unwell, and dull in spirits, and I was more than usually unsuspicious of accident. After a walk, and a very gentle gallop, I brought him to water. Our watering troughs stood by a pump under the Devil's Ditch, on the side next to Newmarket. Not foreseeing any possible danger, I held the reins quite slack, and did not sit upright in my seat, but rested on one thigh; when suddenly, without any warning, a grey rook, of the species common to that plain, ascended on the wing up the ditch within half a yard of the ground, and in a direction that would scarcely have missed the horse's head. At this sudden apparition, an arrow from a bow could hardly exceed the velocity with which he darted round to avoid his enemy; and the impulse was so unforeseen, and so irresistible, that I and my whole stock of self-confidence, and self-conceit, lay humbled in the dust. I was greatly afraid, lest my disgrace should be witnessed by any one, and particularly that the horse should make for home: however, his fright ceasing, and his health not disposing him to be wanton, he easily suffered himself to be caught, and mounted, and my honour received no stain.

I felt this accident the more, because I was at this very time receiving new marks of confidence in my talents. A horse bred in Ireland had been brought into our train: John Watson did not think proper to let a boy of heavy weight back him, and among those of light weight, I was the only one in whom he durst confide. It was for this horse that I quitted the Dun horse, on whose back I had obtained such praise, and upon him the other boy of the name of Tom was mounted, but only for two or three mornings. Dun immediately discovered he was Tom's master, and would not keep up in the gallop, but would go what pace he pleased: if struck, he began to plunge, kick, and rear, threw his rider, and made all the boys laugh and hoot at him, and thoroughly exposed him to mortification.—I was frequently obliged to change my horse, but it was always for one more difficult to manage; and not only so, but I generally preserved an honour that had been early conferred on me, that of leading the gallop, let me ride what horse I would. At one of these changes I was transferred to the back of a little mare, which had long been ridden by Jack Clarke, who was wanted for a horse of more power, but of less spirit. On her too I led the gallop. She was not so much vicious as full of play. Whenever I pleased, when the gallop was begun, by a turn of the arm and a pretended flourish, I could make her start out of the line, clap her head between her legs, fling her hind heels in the air, and begin to cut capers. This excitement was generally sufficient for the whole string, who would start off one after another, each playing his gambols, and perhaps, one or two of them throwing their riders. Under such a temptation for triumph, I was perhaps as prudent as could be expected from a boy of my age; but when John Watson did not happen to be with us, I could not always resist the vanity of shewing that I was equal to the best of them, and quite before the majority. When John was absent, the bad riders would sometimes, before I began the gallop, very humbly intreat me not to play them any tricks; and when they did, I was good-natured enough to comply.

In every stud of horses, there are frequent changes; and as their qualities are discovered, one horse is rejected, and a colt or perhaps a stranger bought and admitted. It happened on such an occasion, that a little horse was brought us from another stud, whence he had been rejected for being unmanageable.

He had shewn himself restive, and besides the snaffle, was ridden in a check-rein. I was immediately placed on his back, and what seemed rather more extraordinary, ordered to lead the gallop, as usual. I do not know how it happened, but under me he shewed very little disposition to be refractory, and whenever the humour occurred, it was soon overcome: that he was however watchful for an opportunity to do mischief, the following incident will discover. Our time for hard exercise had begun perhaps a fortnight or three weeks. As that proceeds, the boys are less cautious, each having less suspicion of his horse. I was leading the gallop one morning, and had gone more than half the way towards the foot of Cambridge hill, when something induced me to call and speak to a boy behind me; for which purpose I rather unseated myself, and as I looked back, rested on my left thigh. The arch traitor no sooner felt the precarious seat I had taken, than he suddenly plunged from the path, had his head between his legs, his heels in the air, and exerting all his power of bodily contortion, flung me from the saddle with only one foot in the stirrup, and both my legs on the off side. I immediately heard the whole set of boys behind shouting triumphantly, " A calf, a calf!" a phrase of contempt for a boy that is thrown. Though the horse was then in the midst of his wild antics, and increasing his pace to full speed, as far as the tricks he was playing would permit, still finding I had a foot in the stirrup, I replied to their shouts by a whisper to myself, " It is no calf yet." The horse took the usual course, turned up Cambridge hill, and now rather increased his speed than his mischievous tricks. This opportunity I took with that rashness of spirit which is peculiar to boys; and notwithstanding the prodigious speed and irregular motion of the horse, threw my left leg over the saddle. It was with the utmost difficulty I could preserve my balance, but I did: though by this effort I lost hold of the reins, both my feet were out of the stirrups, and the horse for a moment was entirely his own master. But my grand object was gained: I was once more firmly seated, the reins and the stirrups were recovered. In a twinkling, the horse, instead of being pulled up, was urged to his utmost speed, and when he came to the end of the gallop, he stopped of himself with a very good will, as he was heartily breathed. The short exclamations of the boys at having witnessed what they thought an impossibility, were the gratification I received, and the greatest, perhaps, that could be bestowed.

I once saw an instance of what may be called the grandeur of alarm in a horse. In winter, during short exercise, I was returning one evening on the back of a hunter, that was put in training for the hunter's plate. There had been some little rain, and the channel always dry in summer, was then a small brook. As I must have rubbed his legs dry if wetted, I gave him the rein, and made him leap the brook, which he understood as a challenge for play, and beginning to gambol, after a few antics he reared very high, and plunging forward with great force, alighted with his fore-feet on the edge of a deep gravel-pit half filled with water, so near that a very few inches further he must have gone headlong down. His first astonishment and fear were so great, that he stood for some time breathless and motionless: then, gradually recollecting himself, his back became curved, his ears erect, his hind and fore leg in a position for sudden retreat; his nostrils from an inward snort burst into one loud expression of horror; and rearing on his hind legs, he turned short round, expressing all the terrors he had felt by the utmost violence of plunging, kicking, and other bodily exertions. I was not quite so much frightened as he had been, but I was heartily glad when he became quiet again, that the accident had been no worse. The only little misfortune I had was the loss of my cap, and being obliged to ride back some way in order to recover it.

Among the disagreeable, and in some degree dangerous accidents that happened to me, was the following. We had an old grey blood gelding touched in his wind, called Puff, on which John Watson generally used to ride. He had some vicious tricks, and the thing that made him dangerous was, that, in the jockey's phrase, he had lost his mouth, that is, the bit could make no impression on him, and he could run away with the strongest rider: but the whim did not often take him. The watering troughs were filled once a day, and as they were about a mile and a half distant, each lad performed that duty in turns, being obliged to walk for that purpose to the Devil's Ditch and back. One day, when it was my turn, old Puff being in the stable, John Watson allowed me to shorten my task by a ride, of which I was very glad, and Puff was soon brought out. For the office of filling the troughs, it was necessary to take a pail, and accordingly I flung one with the rim over my right shoulder, and under my left arm, as was the way with us when we walked. then mounted, but had not gone far, before I found Mr. Puff was determined on one of his frolics. He set off at a good round gallop. This I should not have regarded in the least, had it not been for the pail at my back. But he was a tall horse, the ruts before the race-course began were numerous, rough, and often narrow, and he amused himself with crossing them; so that the rim of the pail was very disagreeable, and now and then hurt my back severely. I foresaw, however, that my only remedy was to tire him out at his own diversion. As soon, therefore, as I had an opportunity, I turned him upon the turf, by which I avoided the worst jolts of the pail; and instead of struggling with him, I gave him head, hurried him forward as fast as he could go, passed along the side called the flat, turned in beside the Devil's Ditch, forbore to push him when we came to the watering troughs, but found the obstinate old devil was resolved not to stop. I then took him full gallop up Cambridge hill, and into Newmarket, supposing his own home would satisfy him. But no! away he went into the town, while some boys belonging to other stables exclaimed, "Here is old Puff running away with Watson's Tom." At a certain distance down the main street, was a street on the left, by which making a little circle, I might again bring his head homewards, and that road I prevailed on him to take; but as he was not easily guided, he thought proper to gallop on the causeway, till he came to a post which bent inwards towards the wall, so much that it was doubtful whether his body would pass. He stopped short at a single step, but luckily I had foreseen this, or I should certainly have been pitched over his neck, and probably my back would have been broken, had I not employed both hands with all my force to counteract the shock. Having measured the distance with his eye, he saw he could pass, which to me was a new danger: my legs would one or both of them have wanted room, but with the same juvenile activity, I raised them on the withers, and away again we went, mutually escaping unhurt. By this time, however, my gentleman was wearied; in two minutes we were at home, and there he thought proper once more to stop. The worst of it, however, was, that I had still to water my troughs. I shall conclude this chapter with a fact which may deserve the attention of the philosopher, as an instance of deep feeling, great sagacity, and almost unconquerable ambition among horses; and which goes nearly to prove, that they themselves understand why they contend with each other. I have mentioned a vicious horse, of the name of Forester, that would obey no boy but Tom Watson: he was about ten or eleven years old, and had been a horse of some repute, but unfortunately his feet foundered, for the cure of which he was suffered to remain a great part of his time at grass. However, when I had been about a year and a half at Newmarket, Captain Vernon thought proper to match him against Elephant, a horse belonging to Sir Jennison Shaftoe, whom by the bye I saw ride this famous match. Forester, therefore, had been taken up, and kept in training a sufficient time to qualify him to run this match; but it was evident that his legs and feet were far from being in that sound state which such an exertion required, so that we concluded he must be beaten, for the reputation of Elephant arose out of his power rather than his speed. Either I mistake, or the match was a four mile heat over the strait course; and the abilities of Forester were such, that he passed the flat, and ascended the hill as far as the distance post, nose to nose with Elephant; so that John Watson who rode him began to conceive hopes. Between this and the chair, Elephant, in consequence of hard whipping, got some little way before him, while Forester exerted every possible power to recover at least his lost equality; till finding all his efforts ineffectual, he made one sudden spring, and caught Elephant by the under-jaw, which he griped so violently as to hold him back; nor was it without the utmost difficulty that he could be forced to quit his hold. Poor Forester, he lost; but he lost most honourably! Every experienced groom, we were told, thought it a most extraordinary circumstance. John Watson declared he had never in his life been more surprised by the behaviour of a horse.

CHAP. XV.

"THE feature in my character which was to distinguish it at a later period of life, namely, some few pretensions to literary acquirement, has appeared for a time to have lain dormant. After I left Berkshire, circumstances had been so little favourable to me, that, except the mighty volume of Sacred Writ (which I always continued more or less to peruse, wherever I found a Bible) and the two small remnants of romance I have mentioned, letters seemed to have lost sight of me, and I of letters. Books were not then, as they fortunately are now, great or small, on this subject or on that, to be found in almost every house: a book, except of prayers, or of daily religious use, was scarcely to be seen but among the opulent, or in the possession of the studious; and by the opulent they were often disregarded with a degree of neglect which would now be almost disgraceful. Yet in the course of six or seven years, it can hardly be imagined that not a single book fell in my way; or that if it did, I should not eagerly employ such opportunity as I had to know its contents. Even the walls of cottages and little alehouses would do something; for many of them had old English ballads, such as Death and the Lady, and Margaret's Ghost, with lamentable tragedies, or King Charles's golden rules, occasionally pasted on them. These were at that time the learning, and often, no doubt, the delight of the vulgar. However, I may venture to affirm, that during the period we have passed, I neither had in my possession, nor met with any book of any kind which I had leisure and permission to read through. During my residence at Newmarket, I was not quite so much in the desert, though, as far as my limits extended, I was little removed: a tolerable estimate of the boundary may be formed from the remaining chapters of this book.

Whether I had or had not begun to scrawl and imitate writing, or whether I was able to convey written intelligence concerning myself to my father for some months after I left him, I cannot say, but we were very careful not to lose sight of each other; and following his affection, as well as his love of change, in about half a year he came to Newmarket himself, where he at first procured work of the most ordinary kind at his trade. There was one among his shop-mates whom I well remember, for he was struck with me and I with him: he not only made shoes, but was a cock-feeder of some estimation; and what was to me much more interesting, he had read so much as to have made himself acquainted with the most popular English authors of that day. He even lent me books to read: among which were Gulliver's Travels, and the Spectator, both of which could not but be to me of the highest importance. I remember after I had read them, he asked me to consider and tell him which I liked best: I immediately replied, "there was no need of consideration, I liked Gulliver's Travels ten times the best." "Aye," said he, "I would have laid my life on it, boys and young people always prefer the marvellous to the true." I acquiesced in his judgment, which, however, only proved that neither he nor I understood Gulliver, though it afforded me infinite delight. The behaviour of my father, who being at work, was present at this, and two or three other dialogues in which there was a kind of literary pretension, denoted the pride and exultation of his heart. He remarked, "that many such boys as Tom were not to be found! It was odd enough! He knew not where Tom had picked it up, he had never had a brain for such things; but God gave some gifts to some, and others to others, seeing He was very bountiful: but, if he guessed rightly, He had given Tom his share!" My father was not a little flattered to find that the cock-feeder was inclined to concur with him in opinion. I remember little else of my literary cock-feeder; yet the advantages I had gained from him in letting me know there were books like these, and introucing me, though but to a momentary iew of Swift and Addison, were perhaps incalculable.

That love of the marvellous which is natural to ill-informed man, is still more lively in childhood. I used to listen with the greatest pleasure to a tale of providential interference; my blood thrilled through my frame at a story of an angel alighting in a field, walking up to a worthy clergyman, telling him a secret known only to himself, and then persuading him to change his road, by which he avoided the murderers that were lying in wait for him. Yet I know not how it happened, but even at this time I refused to believe in witches; and when stories of hobgoblins, of houses that were haunted, or of nightly apparitions were repeated, I remained incredulous. I had either invented or heard some of the plain arguments which shewed the absurdity of such opinions. It will be seen in the following chapter, that my incredulity in this respect was of use to me, though I cannot account for the manner in which I came by it at so early an age.

Books of piety, if the author were but inspired with zeal, fixed my attention whenever I met with them: "the Whole Duty of Man" was my favourite study, and still more Horneck's "Crucified Jesus." I had not yet arrived at Baxter's "Saint's Everlasting Rest," or "The Life of Francis Spira;" but John Bunyan I ranked among the most divine authors I had ever read. In fact I was truly well-intentioned, but my zeal was too ardent, and liable to become dangerous.

One day as I happened to be passing the church, I heard voices singing, which exercise I admired; and having, as I thought, a tuneful voice, I was desirous of becoming acquainted with so pleasing an art. I approached the church door, found it open, and went in, when I found my ear charmed with some heavenly addition to the sweet melody of music; and on inquiry was told, they were singing in four parts. At the head of them was a Mr. Langham, who could sing in a feigned soprano's voice, and who was their instructor in music; for they were all acknowledged learners except himself, and each of them paid him five shillings a quarter for his trouble in teaching them. Having stood with delight to listen some time, a conversation at length began, I was invited to try my voice, and after a ready compliance, both my voice and ear were pronounced to be good. Thus encouraged, I ventured to ask if I might come among them; and was answered, yes; they should be very glad to have me, for they much wanted a treble voice, and all they required was that I should conform to the rules of the society. I inquired what those rules were, and was told, they each paid five shillings entrance, and five shillings a quarter to Mr. Langham, another five shillings for Arnold's Psalmody; and that they paid forfeits of pennies and twopences, if they were absent on certain days, at certain hours, or infringed other necessary bye-laws. An expense so great alarmed me: I would willingly have complied with their forfeits, because I depended on my own punctuality; but fifteen shillings was a vast sum, and I told them what it was that made me hesitate. As they were desirous to have me, they agreed that I should sing out of their books; and Langham, who had great good-nature, said, since I was but a boy, and my wages could not be great, he would give up the entrance money. It was therefore agreed, that with the payment of five shillings a quarter to Mr. Langham, I should be instructed by him in the art of psalmody.

From the little I that day learned, and from another lesson or two, I obtained a tolerable conception of striking intervals upwards or downwards; such as the third, the fourth, and the remainder of the octave, the chief feature in which I soon understood, but of course I found most difficulty in the third, sixth, and seventh. Previously however to any great progress, I was obliged to purchase Arnold's Psalmody; and studious over this divine treasure, I passed many a forenoon extended in the hay-loft. My chief, and almost my only difficulty, lay in the impenetrable obscurity of such technical words as were not explained either by their own nature, or by the author in other language. I was illiterate, I knew th language of the vulgar well, but littl more. Perhaps no words ever puzzle poor mortal more than I was puzzle by the words, *major* and *minor keys* I think it a duty, which no one who writes an elementary book ought to neglect, to give a vocabulary of all the words which are not in common use, in the language in which he writes; and to explain them by the simplest terms in that language; or if that cannot be done, by a clear and easy paraphrase. The hours I spent by myself in mastering whatever belonged to notation, and in learning the intervals, occasioned my progress to be so very different from that of the others, that it excited the admiration of them all; and Mr. Langham, the great man whom I then looked up to, declared it was surprising. If any part was out, I heard it immediately, and often struck the note for them, getting the start of Mr. Langham. If he should happen to be absent, he said that I could set them all right; so that by this, and the clearness of my voice, I obtained the nick-name of the sweet singer of Israel.

My quickness at whatever related to reading became so far known, that a man about fifty, who had many years kept a school in Newmarket, made me the offer, if I would become his scholar, to teach me gratis. Thoroughly glad of the opportunity, I thanked him kindly, and instantly complied. The next morning I went to his school, where I saw a number of boys, to whom I was introduced by the master, as one whom they ought to respect. "I'll set him a word of six syllables," said he, "and I'll engage for him that he shall spell it instantly without the least mistake, or without ever perhaps having seen it before. Pray, my boy," said he, "how do you spell Mahershalalashbas?" The boys first stared at a word of so foreign a sound, and next at the immediate readiness with which I spelled it, though it would be difficult to find a word that could puzzle less: however, since they all wondered at me, it was very natural I should wonder at myself, and that I did most assuredly. The master shewed me the first seat as an honour to his school, where he assured me I might remain as long as he could teach me any thing, and he had by no means the character of ignorance. But, poor gentleman, he had another failing, which I could still less pardon; for every afternoon he was to be seen drunk in the streets, and that to such an offensive and shameful degree, that though I was very desirous to gain some little addition to my stock of knowledge, I felt myself so disgraced by my master, that I went but three times to his school.

This plan, however, suggested another. By trade, Mr. Langham was a maker of leather breeches, which were worn through all Newmarket: but he had by some means acquired rather a greater love of knowledge, and more of it than at that period belonged to his station; for I believe he was only a journeyman. Hearing me bewail the opportunity I had lost, and especially that of acquiring the first rudiments of arithmetic, he joined in my regret, saying it was a pity he could not afford to teach me himself for nothing, and that I could not spare another five shillings a quarter out of my wages; otherwise he would have given me one lesson daily between stable-hours. To this proposal, after turning it in my mind, I however agreed. I continued with him three months, and in that time mastered rule after rule so well, as to understand Practice and the Rule of Three. Except what I have already related, these three months, as far as others were concerned, may be truly called my course of education. At the age of two and three and thirty, indeed, when I was endeavouring to acquire the French language, I paid a Monsieur Raymond twenty shillings for a few lessons, but the good he did me was so little that it was money thrown away. At Newmarket I was so intent on studying arithmetic, that for want of better apparatus, I have often got an old nail, and cast up sums on the paling of the stable-yard. The boys prophesied I should go mad; in which sagacious conjecture our old maid and housekeeper, for she was both, joined them.

CHAP. XVI.

"WHILE my music and my arithmetic were thus in some sort confusing my brain, I became not only ashamed of, but alarmed at myself; for being occasionally sent on errands, I found my memory absent, and made several blunders, a thing to which I had been wholly unaccustomed. One day, when John Watson was at home, I was sent only for two things, and forgot one of them, at which I heard him exclaim, without any reproach,—"God bless me, what is come to the boy!" This startled me a little. As however I remember nothing more of the paroxysm, it could not have lasted very long.

My father did not continue long at his trade, and was obliged to seek some other mode of subsistence. For some months during the middle part of the time that I remained as a stable-boy, he had the office at an inn of fetching and carrying the Royston mail; and being afterwards tired of this, he quitted Newmarket for London, leaving me once more with much good advice, and no small degree of regret. I loved my father, and knew his intentions were honest: but almost from infancy, I was aware they were not wise.

I suppose that that property of the mind, which creates certain indistinct forms and imaginary lines in the clear and visible appearances of things, is common to every person of a lively and active fancy, for I have it still; and now that I am old, much more in sickness than in health. I recollect an instance of this, which occurred about the time I am speaking of. The cowardly boys made bargains with each other to go in pairs, when their business called them to different parts of the yard and out-houses after it was dark: I determined always to go by myself. One evening, intending to fetch some hay from a hay-loft, as I was mounting the ladder, an object presented itself, that instantly stopped me. It was a clear moon-light night, and I beheld the perfect face of a man extended on the hay. He must be a stranger, and might be a robber, or person of evil intentions. I had no idea of a ghost; and though alarmed, I reasoned on probabilities. The more I looked, the more thoroughly I was convinced I saw a real face. Still I continued to reason. I was half way up the ladder. If I returned, I must either fabricate a falsehood, or openly declare why, and this would have been cause of triumph to those whose actions betrayed their fears, and of the greater disgrace to me for having assumed a superiority. The man might be a beggar, who had only obtained entrance by some means, that he might rest comfortably: and even if his designs were wicked, they could not be against me, for I had little to lose: so that at last I determined to proceed. As I have said, the light of the moon was bright: it shone into the loft through the holes and crevices of a side hanging door; and I had mounted three steps higher, before the vision totally disappeared, and was replaced by the rude and unmeaning lines of reality. No man was there, consequently no man's face could be seen. This incident was a wholesome lesson: it taught me to think much on the facility with which the senses are deceived, and the folly with which they entertain fear.

The boys, who had paired off as mutual protectors to each other, had left my name-sake Tom, being the odd one, without a mate, and as he was much more remarkable for his cowardice than his valour, the best expedient he could think of was to offer me a half-penny a night if I would go with him in the dark to get his hay. I believe nothing could have made him stir from the fire-side on a winter night, but the fear of neglecting his stable duties, which fear to all of us had something in it that was almost sacred. We had at this time in the stables a very beautiful male tabby cat, as remarkable for his familiarity with the horses and boys, as for his fine colours, symmetry, and strength. He would go through the stable night by night, and place himself on the withers, first of this horse, then of the next, and there familiarly take his sleep, till he had made the whole round. The boys had taught him several tricks, which he very willingly repeated as often as they gave the signal, without taking offence at the rogueries they occasionally practised upon him; so that he was a general favourite with every one, from John Watson even to Old Betty. One evening as I was going with Tom to get his hay, and we approached the stable in which it happened then to be kept, Tom leading the road (for cowards are always desirous to convince themselves they are really valiant), a very sudden, vehement, and discordant noise was heard; to listen to which, Tom's valour was wholly unequal. Flying from the stable, he was at the back-door of the house in a twinkling. I was paid for my courage: pride and curiosity concurred to make me show it, and I remained firm at my post. I stood still, while the noise at intervals was several times repeated. It was the beginning of winter, and at one end of the stable a certain quantity of autumn wheat was stowed. I recollected this circumstance, and after considering some time, at length the truth struck me, and I called, " Come along, Tom, it is the cat and the rats fighting, but they will leave off when they hear us come into the stable." We had neither candle nor lanthorn. It was a maxim with John Watson to trust no such things with boys, whose nightly duty it was to fetch trusses of straw and armfulls of hay; but I entered the stable, gave Tom his hay, loaded myself with my own, and confident in the valour of our favourite cat, said to him —" We shall find a rare number of dead rats to-morrow, Tom." I knew not the power of numbers, nor the imbecility of an individual so exposed. The next morning we found our hero lying dead in the stable, with only three dead rats beside him. What the number of the wounded was, must remain a secret to posterity: though of the value of this, and other secrets of the same kind, I have often entertained my doubts.

John Watson remained a bachelor, and old Betty was the only female, at least that I can recollect, in the family: she was very ignorant, and very angry when boys durst contend with her age and experience, but we did not greatly respect her anger. She was so strenuous an advocate for goblins, apparitions, and especially witchcraft, that she did not in the least scruple to affirm things the most extravagant. One of her positions was, that unthinking old women with less courage and sagacity than herself, were taken by surprise, and made witches against their will. Imps of the devil came slily upon them, run up their clothes, caught some part of the breast in their mouths, and made teat for themselves.

She provoked me very much, yet I could not help laughing; while she, to prove the truth of what she said, affirmed, she had seen them peeping out more than once; and that on a certain night, two of them made a desperate attempt on her, which she could no otherwise defeat, than by taking up first one, and then the other, with the tongs, and throwing them both into the red hot part of the kitchen fire.

Stories like these are almost too ludicrous to be mentioned, but the one I am going to relate, was at that time to me as tragical as any thing that could happen to an individual.

Jack Clarke, now about eighteen, was spending his evening before nine o'clock in his good-natured way among the boys of Lord March, who lived opposite. One of them, (I forget his name), took down a fowling-piece that was hanging over the kitchen chimney, and playing that trick which has been so repeatedly, and in my opinion so strangely played, said, "Now, Jack, I'll shoot you." As he spoke, he pulled the trigger, and the distance between them being short, Clarke was shot on the left side of his face, the middle half of which immediately became as frightful a wound as perhaps was ever beheld. The lads of both stables were there instantly: the grooms came the moment they could be found, and the terror and distress of the scene were very great, for every body felt kindness for Jack Clarke. Tom Watson was dispatched on horseback to Cambridge in search of all the surgical and medical aid that could be obtained; and such was his speed, that the surgeon, the doctor, and himself, were back by midnight, and the medical men busy in probing, inquiring, and consulting, while poor Clarke lay groaning, extended on the bed of John

Watson. The left cheek-bone, eye, and other parts, were shattered past hope: the case was thought precarious, there was a bare possibility that the patient, miserable as he was, and shocking to look at, might survive. When the physician and surgeon had done all that they could by dressing and giving orders, John Watson took them under his care for the night. Whether he found beds and entertainment for them at an inn, or at the house of a friend, I know not; but as I saw him no more, I suppose he remained with them to keep them company, for such scenes do not immediately dispose the mind to sleep. Among ourselves at home, however, a very serious question arose, no less than that of, who should sit up and watch with him all night? His sufferings were so incessant, his groans so terrifying, and the wounds (by which the inside of the head was made visible) had been so bloody, raw, and torn, being at the same time most frightfully spread all round with gun-powder, and black and red spots, that every person present frankly owned they durst not stay alone all night with him in the same chamber. When it was proposed to old Betty, she was in an agony. All the older boys expressed the terror it would give them :—some sleep must be had, and it being winter, the stables were to open before four. What, therefore, could be done? I own I was almost like the rest, but I most truly pitied poor Jack Clarke. I had always felt a kindness for him, and to see him forsaken at so distressing a moment, left by himself in such a wretched state, no one able to foresee what he might want, overcame me, and I said, "Well, since nobody else will, I must!" Besides, by an action so bold, performed by a boy at my age, I gained an undeniable superiority, of which any one of the elder boys would have been proud.—The medical men remained at Newmarket, or went and came as their business required, while Jack Clarke continued under their hands. I was truly anxious for his cure, though from what I had seen on the first night, and from my ignorance in surgery, I had supposed such a thing impossible. I was therefore surprised that he should seem at first to linger on, that afterwards the wounds should fill up, and assume a less frightful appearance, and that at length a perfect cure should be effected. It was certainly thought to do great honour to Cambridge. The left eye was lost, the appearance of the bones was disfigured, and the deep stain of the gun-powder remained. But before I came away appearances varied, the marks of the gun-powder became less; and when I left Newmarket, Jack Clarke had been long restored to the stables, where he continued to live, apparently in good health.

CHAP. XVII.

"DURING these events and accidents, the trifling studies I might be said to have, were, as far as I had the means, pursued. That is, whenever I could procure a book, I did not fail to read it; I took pains to repeat, that I might well understand my rules in arithmetic; and as for music, Arnold was studied with increasing ardour. But the instructions of Arnold were only vocal: nay, they had a stricter limitation, they were confined to psalmody. Had I possessed any instrument, had I begun to practise, and had the means of obtaining a livelihood suggested themselves in this way, music would, most probably, have been my profession.

Moral remarks do not escape the notice of boys whose minds are active, nor the moral consequences of things, so much perhaps as is supposed. They now and then discover how much they are themselves affected by them; and therefore are not only led to re-consider their own, but begin to ruminate on some of the practices of mankind. For myself, I looked up with delight to angelic purity, and with awful reverence to the sublime attributes of the Godhead. The first I considered as scarcely beyond the attainment of man; the second I considered it as the grand reward of saints and angels to be allowed to comprehend. Towards the future attainment of any such angelic perfection, I could not discover the least tendency in the manners of Newmarket, or the practices of the people around me. When left to themselves, petty vulgar vices, such as their means could afford, were common among them: and at the grand periodical meetings of the place, I heard of nothing but cards, dice, cock-fighting, and gambling to an enormous amount.

One anecdote which John Watson, who was no babbler, told his brother Tom, and which Tom was eager enough to repeat, struck me for its singularity and grandeur; as it appeared to me, who then knew nothing of vast money speculations, and who know but little at present. In addition to matches, plates, and other modes of adventure, that of a sweepstakes had come into vogue: and the opportunity it gave to deep calculators to secure themselves from loss by *hedging* their bets, greatly multiplied the bettors, and gave uncommon animation to the sweepstakes mode. In one of these, Captain Vernon had entered a colt or filly; and as the prize to be obtained was great, the whole stable was on the alert. It was prophesied that the race would be a severe one; for, though the horses had none of them run before, they were all of the highest breed; that is, their sires and dams were in the first lists of fame. As was foreseen, the contest was indeed a severe one; for it could not be decided,—it was a dead heat: but our colt was by no means among the first. Yet so adroit was Captain Vernon in hedging his bets, that if one of the two colts that made it a dead heat had beaten, our master would, on that occasion, have won ten thousand pounds: as it was, he lost nothing, nor would in any case have lost any thing. In the language of the turf, he stood ten thousand pounds to nothing.

A fact, so extraordinary to ignorance, and so splendid to poverty, could not pass through a mind like mine without making a strong impression, which the tales told by the boys of the sudden rise of gamblers, their reverses, desperate fortunes, empty pockets at night, and hats full of guineas in the morning, only tended to increase. With my companions I repeated, *Never venture, never win*: and in this state of puerile avarice, I made bets to the amount of more than half my year's wages, the very next day on the race ground, all to be decided within the week. Concerning the event, however, when it was too late, my mind began to misgive me. By each match, in which I had a venture, my fears were increased; for I generally found myself on the wrong side. My crowns and half-crowns were dwindling away; yet in the midst of my despair, I looked with some degree of surprise at myself, and said, "How can these boys with whom I betted, who are so very ignorant, and over whom, even on the turf or in the stable, I feel my own superiority, have so much more cunning in laying bets than I have?"

Like many of the tragical farces of life, this hastily formed scheme of mine was without a basis, formed on confused suppositions, and ending in total disappointment; for at the end of the week, the loss I had sustained was somewhat either over or under a guinea and a half. To me, who never before had ventured to bet sixpence, who now well remembered that all the good books I had read, held gambling in abhorrence;

and who recollected, with unspeakable anguish, that the sin and folly must be told to my father; that, face to face, I must avow what I had done (for how else could I account for the expenditure of money, for which I could find no equivalent?) to me, I say, these were excruciating thoughts, as will be proved by the desperate remedy I attempted. Well was it for me that the races were over, or my little purse would have been wholly emptied. As it was not therefore possible for me to recover my loss in this way, I began to consider whether there was no other, and despair at length suggested another; a wild one, it is true, but no one could deny its possibility. The race week was just over; thousands of pounds had been betted; guineas and purses had passed in multitudes, from hand to hand, and pocket to pocket, over a vast area, extending from the chair to the

Devil's Ditch, and spreading to I know not what width: might not some stray guinea, nay, perhaps some weighty purse, be now lying there for the first fortunate comer? Or rather, was it not a thing exceedingly likely? I could not suppose the seeds of this golden fruit to be sown exceedingly thick, or that it would not require a long search: but I must not spare my labour: such good luck might befal me, and so eager was my mind to rid itself of its present anguish, that I was willing to believe I should be successful.

The next morning the horses were no sooner dressed and fed, and the stables cleaned, than I hurried to execute my design. I began it by a most careful examination of the betting chair, round which I slowly walked a number of times, and finding nothing below, mounted, examined its crevices, and after often attempting to go, and as often lingering by some faint endeavour to renew hope, could not quit it at last, but with painful reluctance. Where should I seek next? The whole heath was before me; but which was the lucky spot? Groups of horsemen had assembled here and there: but to find each individual place? Oh that I had marks by which to discover! —Thus with my eyes fixed on the ground, wandering eagerly in every direction, I slowly paced the ground, wholly intent on the perplexing thoughts and fruitless pursuits, till increasing disappointment, and inquiry into the time of day, sent me back. This experiment of money-finding on Newmarket heath, might be thought sufficient, but, no! I had an hour in the evening: it was a fine moonlight night, and dejected as I was, I resolved again to try, and forth I went, but it was indeed on the forlorn hope. The incident however forcibly paints the nature of my feelings. I could not endure to confess to my father both my guilt, and evident inferiority in cunning to other boys; and to fabricate a lie, was perhaps equally painful. All that remained was to put off the evil day, and come to my account as late as might be. What I mean will be better understood, when it is known I had determined to leave Newmarket, and return to my father, not however without having first consulted him, and gained his approbation. My mind having its own somewhat peculiar bias, circumstances had rather occurred to disgust me, than to invite my stay. I despised my companions for the grossness of their ideas, and the total absence of every pursuit, in which the mind appeared to have any share. It was even with sneers of contempt that they saw me intent on acquiring some small portion of knowledge: so that I was far from having any prompter, either as a friend or a rival. As far as I was concerned with horses, I was pleased; but I saw scarcely a biped, John Watson excepted, in whom I could find any thing to admire.

Having taken my resolution, I had to summon up my courage to give John Watson warning; not that I in the least suspected he would say any thing more than, very well: but he had been a kind master, had relieved me in the day of my distress, had never imputed faults to me, of which I was not guilty, had fairly waited to give my faculties time to shew themselves, and had rewarded them with no common degree of praise when accident brought them to light. It was therefore painful to leave such a master. With my cap off, and unusual awkwardness in my manner, I went up to him, and he perceiving I was embarrassed, yet had something to say, began thus. "Well, Tom, what is the matter now?"—"Oh, Sir, nothing much is the matter: only I had just a word to say,"—"Well, well, don't stand about it; let me hear." —"Nay, sir, it is a trifle; I only came to tell you, I think of going to London."—"To London?"—"Yes, Sir, if you please."—"When do you mean to go to London?"—"When my year is up, Sir."—"To London! What the plague has put that whim into your head?"—"I believe you know my father is in London."—"Well, what of that?"—"We have written together, so it is resolved on."—"Have you got a place?"—"I don't want one, Sir, I could not have a better than I have."—"And what are you to do?" —"I can't tell that yet, but I think of being a shoemaker."—"Pshaw, you are a blockhead, and your father is a foolish man."—"He loves me very dearly, Sir; and I love and honour him."—"Yes, yes, I believe you are a good boy, but I tell you, you are both doing a very foolish thing. Stay at Newmarket, and I will be bound for it, you will make your fortune."—"I would rather go back to my father, Sir, if you please."—"Nay, then, pray take your own way."—So saying, he turned from me with very visible chagrin, at which I felt some surprise; for I did not imagine it would give him the least concern, should any one lad in the stables quit his service.

Spring and summer kept passing away: Arnold continued to afford me difficulties which I continued to overcome: my good-tempered, pleasant friend, (for so he was) the breeches-maker, and I, used often to consult together; and his surprise that I should so soon have gone beyond him with respect to the theory of music, not a little flattered me. The honest psalm-singers were told I was about to leave them, and owned they were sorry to hear it, I gave them so much assistance. In short, such friends as a poor boy of fifteen, wholly unrelated in the town could have, all expressed a degree of regret at parting: my stable-companions were the only persons who expressed no emotion one way or the other. I must here, however, except poor Jack Clarke, who, as he was the first that introduced me to Newmarket, so he was the last, of whom I took leave."

END OF MR. HOLCROFT'S NARRATIVE.

BOOK II.

CHAP. I.

AT the expiration of his year, Mr. Holcroft left John Watson and his associates at Newmarket; and returned, as he had intended, to his father, who then kept a cobler's stall in South-Audley Street. He was at this time near sixteen. He continued to work in the stall with his father, till the latter could afford to pay a journey-man shoe-maker, to instruct him in the business of making shoes, which in time he learned so well, as to obtain the best wages.

From his early childhood, however, he had eagerly read whatever books came in his way, and this habit did not now leave him: so that, though an exceedingly quick workman, it was rarely that he had a shilling to spare, except for absolute necessaries; and when he had, it was spent at an old book-stall, and *his time was again idled away in reading.*—Such was the complaint continually made against him. At nineteen, he travelled to Liverpool with his father, who seems still to have retained his love of wandering, and who was most probably determined in this excursion by a desire to revisit his native country. This happened in the year 1764: and in the year following, Mr. Holcroft married. While he continued at Liverpool, he procured the humble office of teaching children to read, at a small school in the town. But in less than a year, he left the country, and came to London. Here he continued to work at his trade as a shoemaker, yet gleaning knowledge with all the industry in his power. He had advanced as far as fractions in Arithmetic, knew something of geometry, could write a legible hand, and had made himself a complete master of vocal music. But the stooping position required in making shoes brought on a return of his old disorder, the asthma; and as he hated the trade, he made every effort to find out some other employment.

Mr. Holcroft had, through life, except during the time he was at Newmarket, felt the effects of poverty very severely: but they now preyed more upon his mind than his body. He continually ruminated on the advantages that would have resulted from a good education; and the consciousness that he had neither received one, nor could now pay for instruction, gave him the utmost uneasiness. He was not aware that the desultory materials which he had been at so much pains to collect, would at last form themselves into a consistent mass.

It seems however, that at this period he could not resist the inclination he occasionally felt to commit his thoughts to paper: he even found an editor of a newspaper (the Whitehall Evening Post,) who so far approved of his essays, as to pay him five shillings a column for them. One of them was transcribed into the Annual Register: but, according to his own account, it was much too jejune a performance to deserve any such honour. About this time, Mr. Holcroft attempted to set up a day-school somewhere in the country, where for three months he lived upon potatoes and buttermilk, and had but one scholar. At the expiration of the first quarter, he gave up his school, and returned to London. After this, he obtained admission into the family of Mr. Granville Sharpe, with whom he went to reside, partly in the character of a servant, and partly I believe as a secretary. It is not certain, whether he was introduced to the notice of this amiable but eccentric man, by his literary efforts, or by accident. Both before and after he went to live with Mr. S. he had been accustomed to attend a reading-room, or spouting-club, the members of which in turn rehearsed scenes and passages out of plays. His master did not think this the best mode of spending his time, and made some attempts to cure him of what he considered as an idle habit. These however proved ineffectual, and he was at length dismissed from the house of his patron.

He now found himself once more in

the streets of London, without money, without a friend, that shame or pride would suffer him to disclose his wants to, or a habitation of any kind to hide his head in. At last, as he was wandering along wherever his feet led him, his eye accidentally glanced on a printed paper pasted against the wall. This was an invitation to all those spirited young fellows, who chose to make their fortunes as common soldiers in the service of the East India Company. He read it with the greatest satisfaction, and was posting away with all haste to enrol his name in that honourable corps, when he was met by one of the persons, whom he had known at the spouting-club. His companion, seeing his bundle and rueful face, asked him where he was going; to which Holcroft replied, that, had he inquired five minutes sooner, he could not have told him; but that, at present, he was for the wars.

At this his spouting friend appeared greatly surprised, and told him, he thought he could put him upon a better scheme. He said, one Macklin, a famous London actor, was going over to play in Dublin; that he had been inquiring of him for a young fellow, who had a turn for the stage; and that, if Holcroft pleased, he would introduce him; observing that it would be time enough to carry the knapsack, if the sock did not succeed. This proposal was too agreeable to our adventurer to be heard with inattention. Accordingly, having thanked his acquaintance, and accepted his offer, the next day was fixed upon for his introduction to Macklin. The friend, on whom Holcroft had thus unexpectedly lighted, was, in fact, a kind of scout, employed by Macklin, to pick up young adventurers of promising talents: it being one of this actor's passions to make actors of others; though he was in some respects the worst qualified for the office of any man in the world.

The next morning they proceeded to the place of appointment, when they found the great man seated on his couch, which stood by the fire; and on which, whenever he felt himself tired or drowsy, he went to rest, both day and night; so that he sometimes was not in bed for a fortnight together. As they went in, they were followed by his wife, who brought him a bason of tea and some toast, with each of which he found fifty faults in the rudest manner. He afterwards called to her several times, upon the most frivolous occasions, when she was dignified with the style and title of Bess. His countenance, as it appeared to Mr. Holcroft at this interview, was the most forbidding he had ever beheld; and age, which had deprived him of his teeth, had not added to its softness. After desiring the young candidate to sit down, he eyed him very narrowly for some time, and then asked him, *What had put it into his head to turn actor?* The abruptness of the question disconcerted him; and it was some time before he could answer, in rather a confused manner, that he had *taken it into his head* to suppose it was genius, but that it was very possible he might be mistaken. "Yes," said he, "that's possible enough; and by G—d, Sir, you are not the first that I have known so mistaken." Holcroft smiled at his satire, and the other grinned ghastly with his leathern lips; for our tyro had not added to the beauty of his visage by repeating his words. While Macklin was drinking his tea, they talked on indifferent subjects; and as Holcroft did not happen to differ with him, but on the contrary had opportunities of saying several things which confirmed his opinions, he was pleased to allow that he had the appearance of an ingenious young man. When his beverage was finished, he desired him to speak a speech out of some play, which being done, he remarked that he had never in his life heard a young spouter speak naturally, and therefore he was not surprised that Holcroft did not: but, as he seemed tractable, and willing to learn, if he would call again on the morrow, he would hear and answer him further.

When they had descended into the street, Holcroft's companion assured him *it would do*, for that he had met with a very favourable reception; which was indeed the case, considering the character of the person to whom their visit had been paid.

According to the account Mr. Holcroft has left of this extraordinary man, the author of the comedy of the Man of the World, he was born in the century before the last, yet at the time of Mr. Holcroft's application to him (which was in the year 1770) his faculties did not seem in the least impaired. He was said to have been bred in the interior parts of Ireland, and in such utter ignorance, as not to be able to read at the age of forty. The progress, therefore, which he made afterwards, was an astonishing proof of his genius and industry. His body, like his mind, was cast in a mould as rough as it was durable. His aspect and address confounded his inferiors; and the delight he took in making others fear and admire him gave him an aversion to the society of those whose knowledge exceeded his own; nor was he ever heard to acknowledge superiority in any man. He had no respect for the modesty of youth or sex, but would say the most discouraging, as well as grossest things; and felt pleasure in proportion to the pain he gave. It was common with him to ask his pupils, why they did not rather think of becoming bricklayers than players. He was impatient of contradiction to an extreme; and when he found fault, if the person attempted to answer, he stopped him without hearing, by saying, "Ha, you have always a reason for being in the wrong!" This impatience carried him still farther; it often rendered him exceedingly abusive. He could pronounce the words, *scoundrel*, *fool*, *blockhead*, familiarly, without the least annoyance to his nervous system. He indeed pretended to the strictest impartiality, and while his passions were unconcerned, often preserved it: but these were so extremely irritable, that the least opposition was construed into an unpardonable insult; and the want of immediate apprehension in his pupils subjected them to the most galling contempt, which excited despair instead of emulation. His authority was too severe a climate for the tender plant of genius ever to thrive in. His judgment was, however, in general sound, and his instructions those of a master. "In short," says Mr. H. "if I may estimate the sensations of others by my own, those despots, who, as we are told, shoot their attendants for their diversion, are not regarded with more awe than Macklin was by his pupils and domestics." Such is the conclusion of his severe, but apparently faithful portrait of this singular character; and it will be seen in the sequel, that he had sufficient opportunity for rendering it accurate.

Having finished their visit, Holcroft and his friend adjourned to the Black Lion, in Russell Street, which was at that time a place of resort for theatrical people. He here learnt that Mr. Foote was going to take a company to Edinburgh, after the close of the summer season. Being now anxious to secure himself an engagement, and the manner of Macklin having neither prejudiced him much in his favour, nor given him any certain hopes of success, he resolved to apply to Mr. Foote. Accordingly, making some slight excuse to his companion, he hastened into Suffolk Street.

He had the good fortune to find the manager at breakfast with a young man, whom he employed partly on the stage, and partly as an amanuensis. "Well," said he, "young gentleman, I guess your business by the sheepishness of your manner; you have got the theatrical cacoethes, you have rubbed your shoulder against the scene: hey, is it not so?" Holcroft answered that it was. "Well, and what great hero should you wish to personate? Hamlet, or Richard, or Othello, or who?" Holcroft replied, that he distrusted his capacity for performing any that he had mentioned. "Indeed," said he, "that's a wonderful sign of grace. I have been teazed for these many years by all the spouters in London, of which honourable fraternity I dare say you are a member; for I can perceive no stage varnish, none of your true strolling brass lacker on your face."—"No indeed, Sir."—"I thought so. Well, Sir, I never saw a spouter before, that did not want to surprise the town in Pierre, or Lothario, or some character that demands all the address, and every requisite of a master in the art. But, come, give us a touch of your quality; a speech: here's a youngster," pointing to his secretary, "will roar Jaffier against Pierre, let the loudest take both." Accordingly, he held the book, and at it they fell: the scene they chose, was that of the before-mentioned characters in Venice Preserved. For a little while after they began, it seems that Holcroft took the hint Foote had thrown out, and restrained his wrath: but this appeared so insipid, and the ideas of rant and excellence were so strongly connected in his mind, than when Jaffier began to exalt his voice, he could no longer contain himself; but, as Nic. Bottom says, they both roared so, that it would have done your heart good to hear them. Foote smiled, and after enduring this vigorous attack upon his organs of hearing as long as he was able, interrupted them.

Far from discouraging our new beginner, he told him, that with respect to giving the meaning of the words, he spoke much more correctly than he had expected. "But," said he, "like other novices, you seem to imagine that all excellence lies in the lungs: whereas such violent exertions should be used but very sparingly, and upon extraordinary occasions; for (besides that these two gentlemen, instead of straining their throats, are supposed to be in common conversation) if an actor make no reserve of his powers, how is he to rise according to the tone of the passion?" He then read the scene they had rehearsed, and with so much propriety and ease, as well as force, that Holcroft was surprised, having hitherto supposed the risible faculties to be the only ones over which he had any great power.

Mr. Holcroft afterwards displayed his musical talents, which also met with the approbation of Foote; who, however, told him, that as he was entirely inexperienced with respect to the stage, if he engaged him, his salary at first would be very low. He said, it was impossible to judge with certainty of stage requisites, till they had been proved; and that if, upon consideration, he thought it expedient to accept of one pound per week, he might come to him again a day or two before the theatre in the Haymarket shut up; but that if he could meet with a more flattering offer in the mean time, he begged he might be no obstacle.

Mr. Holcroft came away from this celebrated wit, delighted with the ease and frankness of his behaviour, and elated with his prospect of success. But as he had promised Macklin to call again, he did not think it right to fail in his engagement. Accordingly, on his second visit, he gave him a part to read in a piece of which he himself was the author, and which had met with great success. Having finished this task apparently to the satisfaction of the author, the latter paid his visitor so high a compliment, as to read to him some scenes of a comedy, which he was then writing. They were characteristic and satirical, and met with Holcroft's sincere and hearty approbation, which, it may be supposed, did not a little contribute to prejudice Macklin in his favour. He, however, thought himself bound not to act with duplicity; and he therefore told Macklin of the offer he had had from Foote, excusing this second application from the necessity he was under of getting immediate employment. Macklin allowed the force of his excuse, but thought he might do better in Ireland. He inquired if Holcroft had any objection to become a prompter, adding that the office was profitable, and one, for which, from the good hand he wrote, and other circumstances, he might easily qualify himself. Holcroft answered that Macklin was the best judge of his fitness for the office, and that he had no objection to the situation, except that it would be more agreeable to his inclination to become an actor. This inclination the other said might be indulged at the same time, which would render him so much the more useful. Little parts would frequently be wanting; the going on for these would accustom him to face the audience, and tread the stage, which would be an advantage. Holcroft then demanded what salary would be annexed to this office; and received for answer, that, as there was a good deal of trouble in it, he could not have less than thirty shillings a week, especially if he undertook to perform small parts occasionally. Macklin also informed him, that he was not manager himself, he only went as a performer: but that Mr. ——, one of the managers, was in town, to whom he would speak, and in two or three days return him a positive answer. In the interim he desired his *protegé* to call in the morning, and he would give him instructions in the part he had read to him, for he had some thoughts of letting him play it. After making proper acknowledgements for these favours, our young adventurer took his leave, much better pleased than at his first visit.

CHAP. II.

It was not long before every thing was settled in the manner proposed by Macklin, and Mr. Holcroft was informed, that it was necessary for him to set off for Dublin, it being the intention of the proprietors to open the theatre about the beginning of October. In consequence of the desire he had expressed to appear in some character, Macklin had promised not only to procure him such an opportunity, but likewise to instruct and become his patron: and on Holcroft's representing to him his want of cash for the journey, he lent him six guineas on the part of the managers, and gave him a letter to Mr.———, who would, he said, provide him with a lodging, and do him other trifling services, which would be agreeable to a person in his situation.

Holcroft now rewarded his spouting friend with a guinea, redeemed his clothes, which he had been forced to pawn, and left London, elated with the most flattering hopes.—He arrived in Dublin about the latter end of September, 1770. The novelty of the scene, and the vast difference in the economy and manners of the people, made a strong impression on his imagination. The bar at the mouth of the Liffy renders the entrance up that river passable only to ships of small burthen, and to them only when the tide serves. It was low water when the packet arrived at the mouth of the river, and a boat came along-side of the vessel, into which most of the passengers went, rather than wait another tide, and our adventurer among the rest. The river divides the city, and the other passengers were set on shore on the quay; but Holcroft, as directed by his letter, inquired for Capel-Street, which was on the opposite side. Thither, accordingly, he was carried; and his trunk and himself landed in a beer-house. He was rather astonished, when the watermen demanded five and five-pence, together with a quart of three-penny, for his conveyance from the packet: and the more so, as he had seen the other passengers give but a shilling each, and one or two of the meaner among them only six-pence. He remonstrated against the imposition, and quoted the precedent of the shilling; but in vain.

The disorder of their looks, the smoothness of their tongues, and the possession they had taken of his trunk, on which one of them seated himself, while the other argued the case, induced our novice to comply with their demands: but what gave him the greatest astonishment was, that the landlord of the beer-house, who had sworn stoutly to their honesty, while he was paying them, no sooner saw their backs turned, than, according to his own phraseology, "he pitched them to the *divel,* for a couple of cut-throat, *chating* rascals, that *desarved* hanging worse than a murderer."

The reflections to which this and

similar scenes gave rise in Mr. Holcroft's mind, though trite, are not the less worthy of attention. He says, "During my short stay in Ireland, I had but too many occasions to observe a shocking depravity of manners, which I attribute either to the laws, or the want of a due enforcement of them. The Irish are habitually, not naturally licentious. They have all that warmth and generosity which are the characteristics of the best dispositions; and when properly educated, are an honor to mankind. Ireland has produced many first-rate geniuses; and in my opinion, nothing but the foregoing circumstance has prevented her from producing many more. It is the legislature which forms the manners of a nation."

When our traveller set out from London, he was assured that the house would open in the beginning of October, but it was November before the season commenced; so that his finances were once more exhausted, and he was obliged to apply to the friend to whom Macklin had recommended him, for a farther supply. The acting manager was one D———, a busy, bustling fellow, void of all civility, who pretended to carry the world before him.

Mr. Holcroft soon discovered that there was an insurmountable antipathy between this man's disposition and his own. But the means of his subsistence were at stake; he endeavoured, therefore, to accommodate himself to the other's temper as much as possible, and waited for the arrival of Macklin with the utmost impatience. He understood that his engagement had been permanently fixed at thirty shillings a week: but, when he went to the treasury, he found it reduced to a guinea; and whenever he pleaded his engagement, received the most mortifying and insulting answers. He discovered the entire improbability of his becoming a favourite. None were such but those who could administer the grossest flattery, and who industriously listened to whatever was said in the theatre concerning this petty despot and his management, in order to repeat it in the ear of their employer.

Holcroft had vainly imagined that the presence of Macklin would put an end to all his grievances: he looked up to him as his patron, as one who had been the occasion of his leaving England, who had pledged himself to be his friend, and was bound to protect him. Whether D—— had prejudiced him against Holcroft, or whether Macklin himself was aware of his deficiency in the honeyed arts of adulation, he could not determine; but he found him very cold in his interest, and far more disposed to browbeat than countenance him. He had, as we have seen, promised to teach him a part, and bring him out in it; but when he ventured to remind him of it, he received only sarcastic remarks on his incapacity. Holcroft, however, persisted in asserting the positiveness of his agreement with respect to his salary, concerning which Macklin had the meanness to equivocate; but he succeeded in obtaining an addition of four shillings a week.

Unable to extricate himself, he endured the insults of malice and ignorance for five months, till the money which he had borrowed had been deducted from his stipend, and then D——— immediately discharged him. It would be no easy task to describe what he must have felt at this moment: he was not possessed of five shillings in the world, was in a strange country, and had no means, now that he was shut out from the theatre, of obtaining a livelihood. He saw nothing but misery and famine before him, and he uttered the bitterest exclamations against Macklin for the perfidiousness of his conduct. This he felt so strongly, that though Macklin by the severity of his manner had gained an almost entire ascendancy over him, he went to his house, and with the utmost firmness, after observing that he would rather starve than incur any farther obligations to him, displayed the impropriety and injustice of his conduct in such animated terms, that all his wonted sternness fled, and the cynic stood abashed before the boy.

There was another theatre open in Smock-Alley, under the direction of Mossop: but he was insolvent, and none of his people were paid. Here, however, as a last resource, Holcroft applied, and was engaged at the same nominal salary that he had in Capel-Street.

It soon appeared that there was no probability of his being paid for his performance at Mossop's theatre: he was therefore forced to quit Dublin, and went on board the Packet for Park-gate, in March, 1771.

The wind was fair till they had lost sight of the hill of Hoath; but soon after sun-set, a hurricane came on, which in this narrow and rocky sea, put their lives in imminent danger. Of this, however, from the violent effects of the sea-sickness, Holcroft was insensible. They were driven during the storm, considerably to the north; and such was the ignorance of the master and, his two or three superannuated mariners, that he still continued sailing to the northward, having no knowledge of navigation, but what he had gained by coasting between the two kingdoms. He was therefore on the present occasion quite at a loss; so that in all probability they might have made a voyage to Greenland, had not an intelligent Scotchman among the passengers known some of the headlands in his own country. The master would have contested the point, but that the passengers perceived his want of skill, and joined the North-Briton, who with a degree of warmth expressive of his attachment to his bleak hills, exclaimed, "What the de'el, mon, d'ye think I dinna ken the craig of Ailsa?"

They were eight days without putting into any port, except sending the boat on shore on the evening of the seventh at the Isle of Man, to procure some provisions for the passengers, who were almost starving, having consumed the stock, which is usually provided for voyages of this kind, in a day or two after the storm had abated. The reason of their being kept so long from port was the dead calm which had succeeded; and which the mariners, who are the most superstitious of all beings, attributed to there being some Jonas on board. This opinion they inculcated among the poor Irish who had paid half a crown for their passage in the hold; who were as ignorant as themselves, and much more mischievous. Unluckily, Holcroft was the person on whom their suspicions lighted. They had discovered him to be a player, a profession, which was at one time regarded by the universal consent of mankind as altogether *profane*. The common Irish in the hold were chiefly catholics, and the sixth day from their departure happened to be Easter-Sunday. Holcroft had sauntered off the quarter-deck, with a volume of Hudibras in his hand, and had walked to the other end of the vessel, when he found himself encircled by two or three fellows with most ferocious countenances, who were gazing earnestly at him, with looks expressive of loathing and revenge. Most of the passengers were at breakfast, and there was no one on deck but these men, and a couple of the sailors, who joined them. The peculiarity of their manner excited his notice, and one of them asked him, his lips quivering with rage, " If he had not better be getting a prayer-book, than be reading plays upon that blessed day?" Holcroft now perceived that the fellows were inebriated, and very imprudently, instead of soothing them, asked them if they imagined there was as much harm in reading a play as in getting drunk on that day, and so early in the morning. " By the holy father," replied the spokesman, " I know you. You are the Jonas, and by Jasus the ship will never see land till you are tossed over-board, you and your plays along with you: and sure it will be a great deal better that such a wicked wretch as you should go to the bottom, than that all the poor innocent souls in the ship should be lost." This speech entirely disconcerted him. The fellow's resolute tone, and the approbation which his companions discovered, were alarming. He, however, preserved presence of mind enough to assure them, it was not a play-book that he was reading, and opened it to convince them, while he slunk away to the quarter-deck, which he gained not without the greatest difficulty. Mr. Holcroft arrived at Chester without any farther accident.

CHAP. III.

Mr. Holcroft had now the world once more before him; and he resolved to write to such travelling companies as he could obtain any intelligence of. His knowledge of music, his talents as a singer, and his recent arrival from the Dublin theatre, were recommendations which procured him the offer of several engagements. He closed with one, in a company that was then at Leeds in Yorkshire. In this his evil fortune was again predominant. He found the affairs of the company in a state of the greatest disorder: the players were despised in the town, and quarrelling with one another and the manager. Here, however, he discovered how necessary practice is to the profession of a player;

and perceived that, though some of his new associates could scarcely read, they could all, from the mere force of habit, speak better on the stage than he could.

In a few weeks, in consequence of continual bickerings and jealousies, most of the players deserted the manager; and no others coming to supply their places, the company dissolved of itself. A letter had followed our luckless hero from Chester, inviting him to join another set of actors, then at Hereford: but this had been written nearly a month; it was a hundred and sixty miles across the country, and he did not know, if he set out, whether he should find them there; or if he did, whether they might now stand in need of his assistance. But his money was by this time reduced so low, that it was necessary to come to an immediate determination. With a heavy heart, then, and a light purse, did he begin another journey: and on the fifth day, entered an inn by the road-side, which was eight-and-twenty miles from Hereford, with the sum of nine-pence in his pocket; and in the morning made his exit pennyless. The fatigue he had already undergone, and the scanty fare he had allowed himself, had so reduced his spirits, that he found considerable difficulty in performing this last day's journey on an empty stomach: but there was no remedy. About four o'clock he ascended the hill that looks down upon that ancient city, at the sight of which a thousand anxieties took possession of his bosom. He inquired of the first person he met, with an emotion not easily to be expressed, if the comedians had left Hereford; and to his great joy, was answered that they had not. Faint, weary, and ready to drop with hunger, he traversed the town to inquire for the manager: but it was one of the nights on which they did not perform, and the manager was not to be found. He was then directed to his brother, who was a barber in the place; and upon the family's observing his weakness, and desiring to know if he was not well, he collected courage enough to tell them that he was greatly fatigued, having come a long journey, and for the last day not having broken his fast, except at the brook. Notwithstanding this confession, in making which he had evidently done great violence to his feelings, they heard it without offering him the least refreshment, or so much as testifying either surprise or pity; and he left the house with tears in his eyes. When the players understood that a fresh member was come to join them, they, from sympathy, very soon discovered his situation; and were not a little incensed at the story of the barber.

The company into which Mr. Holcroft was now introduced was that of the Kembles: the father of Mrs. Siddons was the manager. Mr. H. continued with this company some time; and in the course of their peregrinations he visited Ludlow, Worcester, Leominster, Bewdly, Bromsgrove, and Droitwich; in all which places he acted inferior parts. One of the actors in this company, of the name of Downing or Dunning, seems to have made a pretty strong impression on Mr. H.'s fancy, for he has left a very particular description of him. This stage-hero had a large, red, bottle-nose, with little intellect; but he was tall, looked passably when made up for the stage, and had a tolerable voice, though monotonous. To hide the redness of his nose, it was his custom to powder it: but unluckily he drank brandy; the humour that flowed to his nose, made it irritable, and in the course of a scene the powder was usually rubbed off. His wife stood behind the scenes with the powder-puff ready, and exclaimed when he came off—"Lord! Curse it, George! how you rub your poor nose! Come here, and let me powder it. Do you think Alexander the Great had such a nose? I am sure Juliet would never have married Romeo with such a bottle-nose. Upon my word, if your nose had been so red, and large, when you ran away with me from the boarding-school, I should never have stepped into the same chaise with you and your journeyman captain, I assure you." George seldom made any reply to these harangues, except "Pshaw, woman," or by beginning to repeat his part.

In the year 1798, when Mr. Holcroft spent an evening with old Mrs. Kemble, and talked over past times with her, she gave a whimsical picture of this wife of Downing. Mrs. D. was addicted to drinking, exceedingly nervous, and snuffled when she spoke. She used to tell her own story as follows: "He calls himself Downing, Ma'am, but his name is Dunning. I was a quaker, Ma'am, when he first knew me, and put to a boarding-school. He and one Chalmers (I suppose you have heard of that Chalmers, he gave himself the title of Captain)—Well, Ma'am, while I was at the boarding-school, they came a courting to me. Dunning, my husband, that you see there, was a tall, handsome fellow enough; he had not such a bottle-nose then, Ma'am, nor such spindle legs; so he put on a coat edged with gold lace, I don't know where he got it, and gave himself the airs of a gentleman. He thought I was a great fortune ; but, God help me, I had not a shilling ; and I believed him to be what he pretended, when all the while he was no better than a barber ; and this Captain Chalmers was his journeyman. So they persuaded me, innocent fool, to run away with them, thinking they had got a prize, and I thought the same ; so the biter on both sides was bit. So that is the history, Ma'am, of me and Mr. Dunning."

This maudlin lady was often employed to receive the money at the play-house door, and was suspected of petty embezzlements to supply herself with liquor. Mr. Holcroft used sometimes to rally her a little unmercifully on her love of the bottle, and the adventure of the Captain. The dialogue is somewhat coarse, but it may serve as a sample of the tone of conversation which prevailed in provincial companies at that time. "It is very cold to night, Mrs. Downing,"—" Yes, sir,"—" I hope you take care to keep yourself warm."—"What do you mean, sir?"—" Flannel and a little comfort." " What comfort, sir!"—" You know what I mean."—" I know nothing about you, sir!"—" A drop of cordial; lamb's wool is a good lining."—" Gods curse your linings, sir; I know nothing about linings."—" Nay, don't be angry; I have not said you are tipsy." " Gods curse your sayings, sir, I don't care for your sayings. Mr. Downing shall never set foot, after this night, on the same boards with such an impertinent puppy."—" Nay, my dear Mrs. Downing."—" Yes, sir, you are no better; and if George Downing was a man, he would soon teach you good manners."—" He is well qualified, my dear Mrs. D. for he practised upon many a *block-head* before he came to mine."—" And what of that, sir. I understand you; but a barber is as good as a cobbler at any time."

Now it must be allowed, that though there is not much wit or humour in all this, it is very easy and free spoken. Mr. Holcroft was young at the time, and probably ready enough to give into any joke, which he found the common practice of the place.—It may be remarked by the way, that there is a peculiar tone of banter and irony, bordering on ribaldry, which seems almost inseparable from the profession of strolling players. For this many reasons might be given: 1. The contempt (often most undeserved, no doubt) in which they are held by the world, and which they naturally reflect back on one another; for they must soon learn to despise a profession which they see despised by every one else, at least with that single exception which self-love contrives to reserve for us all. 2.

The circumstance that they live by repeating the wit of others, and that they must naturally ape what they live by. In nine instances out of ten, however, this habitual temptation must produce impertinence instead of wit. 3. The custom of repeating things without meaning or consequence on the stage, must lead to the same freedom of speech when they are *off*. It is only acting a part. 4. They have not much else to do, and they assume a certain levity of manner as a resource against *ennui*, as well as to hide a sense of the mortifications and hardships they so often meet with. Lastly, their mode of life, which is always in companies, and in situations where they have an opportunity of becoming acquainted every moment with one another's weak sides, gives rise to a propensity to *quizzing*, as it does in all other open societies; such as of boys at school, of collegians, among lawyers, &c.—But to return to our narrative.

The company of which old Mr. Kemble was the manager, was more respectable than many other companies of strolling players; but it was not in so flourishing a condition as to place the manager beyond the reach of the immediate smiles or frowns of fortune. Of this the following anecdote may be cited as an instance. A benefit had been fixed for some of the family, in which Miss Kemble, then a little girl, was to come forward in some part, as a juvenile prodigy. The taste of the audience was not, it seems, so accommodating as in the present day, and the extreme youth of the performer disposed the gallery to noise and uproar instead of admiration. Their turbulent dissatisfaction quite disconcerted the child, and she was retiring bashfully from the stage, when her mother, who was a woman of a high spirit, and alarmed for the success of her little actress, came forward, and leading the child to the front of the house, made her repeat the fable of the Boys and the Frogs, which entirely turned the tide of popular opinion in her favour. What must the feelings of the same mother have been, when this child (afterwards Mrs. Siddons), became the admiration of the whole kingdom, the first seeing of whom was an event in every person's life never to be forgotten!

It may not be improper to remark in this place, that Mrs. Siddons first appeared in London about the year 1778, without exciting any great notice or expectation. She had acquired her fame in the country, before she was received in 1783 with such unbounded applause on the London theatres. There is a playful and lively letter from Mr. Holcroft to Miss Kemble (most probably Mrs.

Siddons), dated, 12th Feb., 1779, returning her thanks for the favour of her late visit to him while in town, and desiring his remembrances to theatrical friends in the country, and among others, his *Baises Mains* to a Mr. Davis.

A difference with the manager (old Mr. Kemble), occasioned Mr. Holcroft to leave this company; from which he went to that of Stanton, which performed at Birmingham and in the neighbourhood, and sometimes made excursions to the north of England. A memorandum of Mr. Holcroft, dated 1799, gives some account of himself, and of one of his fellow-actors while in this company. "A person called on me of the name of F——, who began by asking if I knew him. I answered no. He replied that it was likely enough, but that we had been acquainted when I was an actor in Walsal, where he played the second fiddle, and doubted not but I should remember that we had often played at billiards together. I answered that I recollected nothing of his person, though I played at billiards with several people, and probably with him. I then asked, which was the best player of the two? He replied that, because he squinted, people thought he could not play; but that, to the best of his recollection, he had won six or seven pounds of me, which greatly distressed me. Yes, said I, the loss of such a sum at that time (in 1773), would have so distressed me, that though I do forget multitudes of things and persons, I think I should not have forgotten such an incident. I was therefore persuaded he was much mistaken in the sum. In answer to this, he said, he had remarked to me at the time we were both upon the same *lay;* and finding I took offence at the expression, he had softened it by saying, we neither of us *wished to lose our money.* He therefore proposed that I should pay him by going halves with him, when he played and betted again. What degree of truth there was in all this, I cannot now exactly tell, only I know that I had a high spirit, and a detestation of all gambling conspiracies, though at that time I played for money and wished to win. I was poor, neither did I then conceive it to be wrong. The man said, he should not have taken the liberty to come to a gentleman *so high in the world* (at this I could not but smile,) as I now was, had not Mr. Clementi told him I was without pride, and entirely free of access. He is a stout man, nearly six feet high, and lives at Birmingham, where he teaches the violin, has daughters, whom he has taught to fiddle, play the harpsichord, &c., and sells music among his scholars. His business in London, he tells me, is to bring up his wife and daughters, and leave them here, the latter for instruction; and that one great motive for visiting me was, to hear Fanny (Miss Holcroft) play. In addition to ungain size, awkwardness, and squinting, he has a clownish gesticulation, and makes such strange contortions of face, as, were it not to avoid giving offence, would excite continual laughter. In talking of billiards, he spoke of a gentleman at Walsal, with whom he used to play, who came with his pockets full of guineas, and that the chinking of these excited in him the most extraordinary desire to win. Here he got up, and gave a picture by gesticulating, squinting, and drawing his muscles awry, of the agitation he used to be in when going to strike the balls. Nothing could exceed the effect of his *naïveté*. The conclusion of his history of Walsal was, that playing at billiards with Stanton, the manager, the latter complained of the largeness of the pockets; to which F—— replied, yes, they were very large, large indeed, as unconscionably large as his four dead shares, added to the five shares he received for the acting of his wife and children; which so affronted Stanton, that he discharged him the next week. He said he left Walsal with thirty pounds in his pocket, which he had won at billiards, promising his wife never to play more, and that he had kept his word. As he appeared to have been the industrious father of a family, I invited him to bring his daughters, and hear Fanny, who did not then happen to be at home; but his left-handed country breeding, or some other motive, made him decline fixing any time."*

* One Keys, who was also a contemporary of

To enable the reader to understand the satirical allusion to the manager's shares, which cost poor F—— his situation as second fiddler in the company, it may be necessary to give a short account of the economy of a provincial theatre. This I cannot do better than by citing Mr. Holcroft's own words. "A company of travelling comedians then is a small kingdom, of which the manager is the monarch. Their code of laws seems to have existed with few material variations since the days of Shakespeare, who is, with great reason, the god of their idolatry.—The person who is rich enough to furnish a wardrobe and scenes, commences manager, and has his privileges accordingly: if there are twenty persons in the com-

Mr. H. in Stanton's company, and has since been a dancing-master, was the father of Mrs. Mills, who played the Spoiled Child, Sophia, in the Road to Ruin, &c.

pany, for instance, the manager includ-ed, the receipts of the house, after all incidental expenses are deducted, are divided into four and twenty shares, four of which are called *dead* shares, and taken by the manager as payment for the use of his dresses and scenes; to these is added the share to which he is entitled as a performer. Our manager (Stanton), has five sons and daughters all ranked as performers; so that he sweeps eleven shares, that is, near half the profits of the theatre, into his pocket every night. This is a continual subject of discontent to the rest of the actors, who are all, to a man, disaffected to the higher powers. They are, however, most of them in debt to the manager, and of course chained to his galley; a circumstance which he does not fail to remind them of, whenever they are refractory.

"They appear to be a set of merry, thoughtless beings, who laugh in the midst of poverty, and who never want a quotation or a story to recruit their spirits. When they get any money, they seem in haste to spend it, lest some tyrant, in the shape of a dun, should snatch it from them. They have a circuit or set of towns, to which they resort when the time comes round; so that there are but three or four in our company who are not well known in *****. I observe that the town's-people are continually railing at them: yet are exceedingly unhappy, if they fail to return at the appointed time. It is a saying among us, that a player's six-pence does not go as far as a town's-man's groat; therefore, though the latter are continually abusing them for running in debt, they take good care to indemnify themselves, and are no great losers, if they get ten shillings in the pound."

This patriarchal manager, with his wife, sons, and daughters, seems to have been not only an object of envy, but from his blunders and stupidity, the butt of the whole company. Among other instances, which are related of his talent for absurdity, he wished to have Shylock in the Merchant of Venice played in the dialect of Duke's Place, and was positive Shakespeare intended it so. He once told the duke in Othello, a messenger was arrived from the *gallows*, instead of the *galleys*; and in playing the part of Bardolph, where that worthy person, descanting on the fieriness of his nose, says, "Behold these meteors, these exhalations," he used to lift his hands to heaven with a solemn flourish, as if he had really seen "the heavens on fire."

CHAP. IV.

WHILE Mr. Holcroft was in this company, or a short time before he entered it, he married again. His second wife was the sister of a Mr. Tipler, of Nottingham: by her he had two children, William, born in 1773, and Sophy, born at Cockermouth, in 1775. Her mother either died in child-bed of her, or shortly after. This marriage would have been a very happy one, had it not been embittered by scenes of continual distress and disappointment, which Mrs. H. bore with a resignation and sweetness of temper, which could not but endear her to a husband of Mr. Holcroft's character. There is a sort of Shandean manuscript of his, written at this time, and in which he gives an account of his own situation, crosses, poverty, &c. In this there are several passages expressive of the tenderest attachment to his wife; and which, from the amiable character he has drawn of her, she seems to have deserved. One of these will, I think, strongly paint the amiableness of his own heart. After describing a series of misfortunes, he breaks out into the following beautiful address to his wife.

"Oh Matilda! shall I ever forget thy tenderness and resignation? Or when in the bitterness of despair, beholding thee pregnant, wan with watching thy sick infant, and sitting assiduously at thy needle to earn a morsel of bread,—when thou hast beheld the salt rheum of biting anguish scald my agonizing cheek, with what tender love, what mild, what sweet persuasive patience, thou hast comforted my soul, and made even misery smile in hope, and fond forgetfulness! Richer than all the monarchs of the east, Matilda, has thy kindness made me: the world affords not thy equal!"

Mr. Holcroft afterwards removed with his wife into Booth's company. She had a good figure, and her husband had taught her to sing, and instructed her sufficiently in the business of the stage to render her serviceable to the theatre. When at Cockermouth in 1775, Mr. Holcroft addressed a letter and a poem to David Garrick, which I shall here insert; both as they are curious in themselves, and are characteristic of the state of his feelings at the time. For the romantic extravagance of his appeal to Garrick's generosity, no other apology seems necessary, than the old adage, that drowning men catch at straws.

To David Garrick, Esq.

SIR,

"I know of no excuse that I can make for the impertinence of this address, but my feelings. They press hard upon me, they are not to be withstood. They have told me your sympathetic heart sighs for the distressed, and weeps with the child of sorrow. I believe they told me truth.

"I am a strolling comedian, have a wife and family, for whom I would fain provide, but have sometimes, notwithstanding the strictest economy, found the task a very difficult one. I am now near three hundred miles from London, in a company that must, in all human probability, soon be dispersed; my wife lying-in at an inn, and in circumstances that I cannot describe. I do not wish to eat the bread of idleness; I neither know, nor wish to know any thing of luxury; and a trifling salary would make me affluent. I have played in the country with applause, and my friends, I am afraid, have flattered me: some of them have ranked me among the sons of genius, and I have, at times, been silly enough to believe them. I have succeeded best in low comedy and old men. I understand music very well, something of French and fencing, and have a very quick memory, as I can repeat any part under four lengths at six hours' notice. I have studied character, situation, dress, deliberation, enunciation, but above all, the eye and the manner; and have so far succeeded, as to be entirely at the head of my profession here in all those characters which nature has any way qualified me for. I am afraid, Sir, you think by this time that I have undertaken to write my own panegyric. That, however, is far from my intention; neither do I wish for employment in any but a very subordinate situation. My wife is a good figure, but her timidity would always place her behind a Queen at your theatre. If you were to find me capable of any thing better than an attendant, to your judgment would I cheerfully accede. If you do not chuse to employ my wife, but would only engage me, I think we should *both* remember it with that enthusiasm of gratitude, with which good minds are oppressed when they receive favours which they have no possible means of returning.

"I am, Sir,

"Your very humble Servant, &c.

"Cockermouth, in Cumberland,
June 1st, 1775, at the house
of George Bowes, hatter.

"P.S. With respect to the trifling Poem inclosed, I meant only to ease my own heart by it: should it reach yours, it will be more than I can expect."

HOPE;

OR,

THE DELUSION.

" Advance, soft soother of the mind,
  Oh! hither bend, a welcome guest:
Sweet Hope! stray hither, here thou'lt find
  Those sanguine thoughts, that please thee best.

Fair Fancy bring, thy darling child,
  Deck'd in loose robes of Alpine white:
With thee, her happy Parent, wild
  She wings her bold, romantic flight.

Blest pair! I'll sing, inspir'd by you,
  Of wealth bestow'd to noble ends,
Of sweet enchanting scenes in view,
  Of future times and faithful friends.

Tho' my sweet William, prattling youth,
  For bread oft begs in accents meek;
Matilda, fairest flower of truth,
  Droops on my breast her dew-dipt cheek.

Tho' the big tears run down my face
  To see her aspect wan and mild,
And hear her lov'd affection trace
  My care-mark'd features in our child.

Tho' fortune lowly bows my neck,
  And cares not for the wretch's groan,—
Yet smile but Hope, or Fancy beck,
  And I'll ascend her star-built throne.

Now, now I mount! Behold me rise!
  Hope lends me strength, and Fancy wings,
Oh! listen to the magic lies,
  Which fleeting, faithless Fancy sings!

With Independence truly blest,
  Of some neat cot she styles me lord,
Where Age and Labour love to rest,
  Where healthy viands press the board.

Now lay me down, kind nymph, at ease
  Beneath yon verdant mountain's brow,
Where wanton zephyrs fan the trees,
  Where violets spring, and waters flow.

What joys—delusive charmer, hold!
  Despair has seiz'd my thick'ning blood:
Her lips how pale! Her cheek how cold!
  Matilda faints for want of food!"

The foregoing stanzas have been given less for the poetry than the history they contain. The distress which they paint did not, it seems, reach Garrick's heart: at least Mr. Holcroft left Cockermouth some time after without having received an answer to his letter. Whether his wife died before or after he left Cockermouth, I do not know; but there is an epitaph on Mrs. Holcroft, written about this period, in which he feelingly laments her loss.

Beauty, Love, and Truth lie here:
  Passenger, a moment stay!
Breathe a sigh, and drop a tear,
  O'er her much-lamented clay.

Death! thy dart is harmless now,
  Widow'd griefs thy stroke defy:
Weak the terrors of thy brow
  To the wretch who longs to die.

At the time that Mr. Holcroft was at Cockermouth, he was in Booth's company, which he had joined at Carlisle in the autumn of 1774. He had just then left Stanton's company, who were performing at Kendal. He was recommended to Booth by a friend of the name of Hatton, who was an excellent comedian, and the hero of the company. He had spoken in high terms of Holcroft's talents, who himself sent off a letter as his *avant-courier*, in which he undertook to do a great deal for very little. He engaged to perform all the old men, and principal low-comedy characters; he was to be the *music*, that is, literally the sole accompaniment to all songs, &c. on his fiddle in the orchestra; he undertook to instruct the younger performers in singing and music, and to write out the different casts or parts in every new comedy; and, lastly, he was to furnish the theatre with several new pieces, never published, but which he brought with him in manuscript, among the rest Dr. Last in his Chariot, which character he himself performed. Here was certainly enough for one man to do; and for all these services, various and important as they were, he stipulated that he should be entitled to a share and a half of the profits of the theatre, which generally amounted to between four and five pounds a night whenever it opened, that is, three times a week. This proposed salary could not, therefore, amount to more than seventeen or eighteen shillings weekly.

In the above list of employments, which Mr. Holcroft undertook to fulfil, the capital attraction, and that which he believed no country manager could resist, was the character of Dr. Last, which he did in imitation of the London performers. The scene in which he produced the most effect was that of the doctor's examination. This, as I have heard it described, was a very laughable, if not a very pleasing performance. Mr. Holcroft was naturally rather long-backed; and in order to give a ridiculous appearance to the doctor, he used to lean forwards, with his chin raised as high as possible into the air, and his body projecting proportionably behind; and in this frog-like attitude, with his eyes staring wide open, and his teeth chattering, he answered the questions that were put to him, in a harsh, tremulous voice, sometimes growling, and sometimes squeaking, and with such odd starts and twitches of countenance, that the effect produced upon the generality of spectators was altogether convulsive. The person who gave me this description said he thought the part a good deal overdone, but that it was a very entertaining caricature. Mr. Holcroft himself went through this part to gratify a friend, a very short time before his death. He said, it always produced a very great effect, whenever he acted it; but that the chief, or only merit it had, was that of being a close imitation of Weston's manner of doing it.*

* Weston is celebrated for his unrivalled power of face, for looking the fool more naturally than any one else. Mr. Holcroft speaks of him in the following manner in the Theatrical Recorder.—"As an actor, I remember him well: to think of a few unrivalled performers, and to forget Weston, is impossible. The range of characters that he personated was confined. The parts in which he excited such uncommon emotion, were those of low humour. He was the most irresistible in those of perfect simplicity: his peculiar talent was the pure personification of nature. I do not think it possible for an actor to be less conscious than Weston appeared to be, that he was acting. While the audience was convulsed with laughter, he was perfectly unmoved: no look, no motion of the body, ever gave the least intimation that he knew himself to be Thomas Weston. Never for a moment was Thomas Weston present; it was always either Jerry Sneak, Doctor Last, Abel Drugger, Scrub, Sharp, or the very character, whatever it was, he stood there to perform; and it was performed with such a consistent and peculiar humour, it was so

The history of the company in which Mr. Holcroft was now engaged, de-

entirely distinct from any thing we call acting, and so perfect a resemblance of the person whom the pencil of the poet had depicted, that not only was the laughter excessive, nay sometimes almost painful, but the most critical mind was entirely satisfied. I doubt if Garrick, or any other actor, had so complete a power of disguising himself, and of assuming a character with so little deviation from the conception he had previously formed. It was not only a perfect whole, but it was also unique.

"He first appeared in tragedy, which he always considered as his forte, though he was utterly unqualified for it. It was much against his will that he was accidentally forced to play Scrub in the Beaux' Stratagem, when he threw every one into raptures, except himself. Even the very boys followed him in the streets, exclaiming, 'There—that's he that played Scrub!' His first appearance in London was at a booth in Bartholomew Fair. He was afterwards engaged by Foote, who was the first person who introduced him to public notice, and who wrote the part of Jerry Sneak expressly for him. Several stories are told of the readiness of his wit, and presence of mind.

serves notice from its singularity. The name of the original founder of

"Shuter had long been the favourite of the galleries; and Weston, before he was well known, appeared as a substitute for Shuter, in the part of Sharp. Shuter's name was in the play-bills; and when Weston appeared, the galleries vociferated, "Shuter, Shuter!" Mrs. Clive played the part of Kitty Pry, and was no less a favourite than the other. The uproar continued, and nothing could be heard but 'Shuter, Shuter!' As soon as it was possible to be heard, Weston, in his own inimitable and humourous manner, asked aloud, in a seriously stupid amazement, and pointing to Mrs. Clive,—'Shoot her! Shoot her! Why should I shoot her? I am sure she plays her part very well!' The apparent earnestness and simplicity with which he asked this question, were so inimitable, and it so truly applied to the excellent acting of Mrs. Clive, that the burst of laughter was universal, and the applause which Weston deserved, attended him through the part.

"Weston was no less remarkable for his dissipation and poverty, than for his comic excellence. It happened on a day that his name was in the play-bills, that he was arrested for a small sum, which he applied to the managers to discharge, the company was Mills, a Scotchman. He and his family had formerly travelled the country, playing nothing but Allan Ramsay's Gentle Shepherd. This they continued to do for several years without either scenery or music. As

which request they refused. Being known to the bailiff, Weston prevailed on him and his follower to go with him to the play, where he placed himself and them in the front of the two-shilling gallery.—Before the curtain drew up, an apology was made, that Mr. Weston, being ill, could not possibly attend; and it was therefore hoped, another performer might supply his place. Weston rose, as he intended, and declared aloud, the apology was entirely false; he was there, well, and ready to do his part, but that he was in custody for a small debt, for which, though entreated, the managers had refused to give security. Weston had well foreseen the consequences: the managers were obliged to set him free. Another actor would have immediately been expelled the theatre; but for Weston no substitute could be found." —Vol. ii. p. 112.

The reason has often been asked, why actors

the younger branches of the family grew up, one of them became a scene-painter, and some of the others learned to fiddle. They now, therefore, added scenes and music to the representation of their favourite pastoral. They afterwards enlarged their circuit, and made excursions into the North of England: and though the loves of Patie and Peggy were a never-failing source of delight on the other side of the Tweed, their English auditors grew tired of this constant sameness. They therefore, after the performance of the Gentle Shepherd, which was

are imprudent and extravagant. An answer may be found in the very nature of their profession. They live in a world of fancy, of artificial life and gaiety, and necessarily become careless of the real consequences of their actions. They make realities of imaginary things, and very naturally turn realities into a jest. Besides, all persons are so, who have no settled prospects in life before them.

still the business of the evening, introduced a farce occasionally, as a great treat to the audience. Mills's daughters married players. This brought an accession of strength into the family, so that they were now able to act regular plays; and by degrees, Allan Ramsay, with his shepherds and shepherdesses, and flocks of bleating sheep, was entirely discarded. Still, however, during the life-time of Mills, the whole business of the theatre, even to the shifting of the scenes, or making up of the dresses, was carried on in the circle of his own family. At his death, the property of the theatre was purchased by a Mr. Buck (formerly of Covent Garden theatre), who kept an inn at Penrith, and it was by him let out to Booth.

Mrs. Sparks, of Drury Lane Theatre, was an actress in this company, at the time Mr. Holcroft belonged to it, and the youngest daughter of Mills, the late manager. Mrs. Inchbald was playing in the same company, at Inverness, in Scotland, in 1773, or the winter of 1774. The company afterwards went to Glasgow, where not being permitted to play, they were all in the utmost distress. The whole stock was detained for rent and board, &c., at an inn. From this awkward situation they were liberated by a young Scotchman, who had just joined the company in a kind of frolic, and who paid their score, and set them off to Kilmarnock, and from thence to Ayr, where they had a very brilliant run of good fortune.

Booth, the manager, was the same person who has since been well known as the inventor of the polygraphic art, and of the art of making cloth without spinning or weaving. He appears to have been always a man of much versatility of enterprise; and at this time added to his employments of manager and actor, the profession of a portrait-painter. The first thing he did when he came to any town, was to wait on the magistrate, to ask leave for his company to play; or if this was refused, that he might have the honour of painting his picture. If his scenes and dresses were lying idle, he was the more busy with his pencil: and that tempting bait hung out at the shop-windows, *Likenesses taken in this manner for half-a-guinea,* seldom failed to fill his pockets, while his company were starving.

CHAP. V.

Mr. Holcroft continued in Booth's company about a year and a half. He next joined Bates's company, which made the circuit of the principal towns on the east side of the north of England, including Durham, Sunderland, Darlington, Scarborough, Stockton-upon-Tees, &c.

It was sometime in the year 1777, that Mr. Holcroft walked with Mr. Shield (the celebrated composer, who was then one of the band in the same company) from Durham to Stockton-upon-Tees. Mr. Holcroft employed himself on the road in studying Lowth's Grammar, and reading Pope's Homer.—The writers that we read in our youth are those, for whom we generally retain the greatest fondness. Pope always continued a favorite with Mr. Holcroft, and held the highest place in his esteem after Milton, Shakspeare, and Dryden. He used often, in particular, to repeat the character of Atticus, which he considered as the finest piece of satire in the language. Moral description, good sense, keen observation, and strong passion, are the qualities which he seems chiefly to have sought in poetry. He had therefore little relish even for the best of our descriptive poets, and often spoke with indifference, approaching to contempt, of Thomson, Akenside, and others. He was, however, at this time, exceedingly eager to make himself acquainted with all our English poets of any note; and he was seldom without a volume of poetry in his pocket.

At the time that Bates's company

were at Scarborough, Fisher, the late celebrated Oboe player, gave concerts there, which were led by Dance, and in which a Miss Harrop, (afterwards Mrs. Bates) was the principal vocal performer. Holcroft used to sing in the choruses.—He at this time practised a good deal on the fiddle, which he continued ever after to do occasionally; but he never became a good performer. It was Bates, who conducted the commemoration of Handel at Westminster Abbey.

Among the parts which Mr. Holcroft played most frequently, were—Polonius, which he did respectably; Scrub, in the Beaux' Stratagem; Bundle, in the Waterman; and Abel Drugger. He acted this last character after he came to London, one night when Garrick happened to be present.

At Stockton-upon-Tees, Mr. Holcroft first became acquainted with Ritson, the antiquarian, and author of the Treatise on animal food, who was afterwards one of his most intimate friends. He was at that time articled to an attorney in the town; but was, like most other young men of taste or talents, fonder of poetry than the law. The poet Cunningham was an actor in the same company. He was the intimate friend of Shield. He was, it seems, a man of a delicate constitution, of retired habits, and extreme sensibility, but an amiable and worthy man. The parts in which he acted with most success were mincing fops and pert coxcombs,—characters the most opposite to his own. He played Garrick's character of Fribble, in Miss in her Teens. He also excelled in Comus. He was often subject to fits of absence; as a proof of which, he once forgot that he had played the Duke of Albany in King Lear, and had returned to the door of the theatre for the second time, before he recollected himself.—Besides his descriptive poems, he wrote several prologues; and an opera called "The Lass with Speech," which was offered to the theatres, but never acted, and from which the Lying Valet was taken. He dedicated his poems to Garrick, who sent him two guineas on the occasion, which he returned, begging that they might be added to the theatrical fund. It seems he either did not want pecuniary remuneration for the compliment he had paid to Garrick, or he thought this a very inadequate one. When he was writing any thing, his room was strewed with little scraps of paper, on which he wrote down any thought as it occurred; and afterwards he had some difficulty in connecting these scattered, half-forgotten fragments together, before he could make out a fair copy.

At the time that Mr. Shield was most with him, he had been long in ill health, apparently in a decline; and this had given a deeper tinge of melancholy to the natural thoughtfulness of his disposition. A little before his death, he wrote the following lines, which seem to convey a presentiment of his fate.

"Sweet object of the zephyr's kiss,
Come rose, come, courted by the hours,
Queen of the banks, the garden's bliss,
Come, and abash yon tawdry flow'rs.
'Why call us to revokeless doom,'
With grief the op'ning buds reply,
'Scarce suffer'd to expand our bloom,
Scarce born, alas! before we die.'

"Man, having pass'd appointed years,
(Years are but days) the scene must close;
And when Fate's messenger appears,
What is he but a withering rose?"

These lines can hardly fail of being acceptable to the reader, when he is told, they were the last ever written by a man, to whom we are indebted for some of the most pleasing and elegant pastoral descriptions in the language.— It must abate something of the contempt with which we are too apt to mention the name of a strolling player, when we recollect that Cunningham was one.

Mr. Holcroft had never been satisfied with his employment as a strolling actor in the country. He sighed for the literary advantages, and literary intercourse which London afforded. He was indeed the whole time labouring hard to cultivate his mind, and acquire whatever information was within his reach. But his opportunities were very confined. He had studied Shakespeare with the greatest ardour, and with some advantage to himself in his profession. Polonius was the character in which he was most successful: he also played

Hamlet, and other parts, of which he was but an indifferent representative. I have been told, that Mr. Holcroft's acting, both in its excellences and defects, more resembled Bensley's than any other person's. The excellent sense and judgment of that able actor were almost entirely deprived of their effect, by his disadvantages of voice and manner. Mr. Holcroft, in the performance of grave parts, had the same distinct, but harsh articulation, and the same unbending stiffness of deportment.

After wandering for seven years as an itinerant actor, with no very brilliant success, he resolved upon trying his fortune in London, and arrived there early in the latter end of 1777. His stay with the last company, which he joined, must therefore have been short. His separation from this company was I believe in some measure hastened by little disagreeable circumstances, but it was no doubt chiefly owing to the general bias of his inclination, to the desire and expectation of fame of some sort or other, either theatrical or literary, on which his mind had for some years been brooding. It is not likely that his success on the stage, though it might in time have ensured him a livelihood in inferior parts, would ever have been such as to satisfy the ambition of an aspiring and vigorous mind. It was however on his talents as an actor, that he first rested his hopes of pushing his fortune in London, and of recommending himself to the favour of the public. But before we follow him up to town, it may not be improper to take a retrospect of the path we have already trod. There are some persons of nice tastes, who may perhaps be disgusted with the meanness of his adventures; and who may think the situation in which he embarked in life, and the society into whose characters and manners he seems to have entered with so much relish, unworthy of a man of genius.

But it should be recollected, first, that men of genius do not always chuse their own profession or pursuit. In Mr. Holcroft's case, the question was, whether he should turn strolling player, or starve.

Secondly, there are in this very profession, which is held in such contempt, circumstances which must make a man of genius, not very averse to enter into it. In spite of the real misery, meanness, ignorance, and folly, often to be found among its followers, the player as well as the poet, lives in an ideal world.

The scenes of petty vexation, poverty, and disappointment, which he has to encounter, are endless; so are the scenes of grandeur, pomp, and pleasure, in which he is as constantly an actor. If his waking thoughts are sometimes disagreeable, his dreams are delightful, and the business of his life is to dream. This may be a reason why every one else should shun this profession as a pest, but it is for this very reason that the man of genius may pass his time pleasantly and profitably in it. But let us hear Mr. Holcroft's apology for his former way of life, which seems to have been dictated with a view to his own feelings. "Know then," he says,* "there is a certain set or society of men, frequently to be met in straggling parties about this kingdom, who by a peculiar kind of magic, will metamorphose an old barn, stable, or out-house, in such a wonderful manner, that the said barn, stable, or out-house, shall appear, according as it

* Hugh Trevor, Vol. iii.

suits the will or purpose of the said magicians, at one time a prince's palace; at another, a peasant's cottage; now the noisy receptacle of drunken clubs, and wearied travellers, called an inn; anon the magnificent dome of a Grecian temple. Nay, so vast is their art, that, by pronouncing audibly certain sentences, which are penned down for them by the head, or master magician, they transport the said barn, stable, or outhouse, thus metamorphosed, over sea, or land, rocks, mountains, or deserts, into whatsoever hot, cold, or temperate region the director wills, with as much facility as my lady's squirrel can crack a nut-shell. What is still more wonderful, they carry all their spectators along with them, without the witchery of broom-sticks. These necromancers, although whenever they please they become princes, kings, and heroes, and reign over all the empires of the vast and peopled earth; though they bestow governments, vice-royalties, and principalities, upon their adherents, divide the spoils of nations among their pimps, pages, and parasites, and give a kingdom for a kiss, for they are exceedingly amorous; yet, no sooner do their sorceries cease, though but the moment before they were revelling and banqueting with Marc Antony, or quaffing nectar with Jupiter himself, it is a safe wager of a pound to a penny that half of them go supperless to bed. A set of poor, but pleasant rogues! miserable, but merry wags! that weep without sorrow, stab without anger, die without dread, and laugh, sing, and dance, to inspire mirth in others, while surrounded themselves with wretchedness. A thing still more remarkable in these enchanters is, that they completely effect their purpose, and make those, who delight in observing the wonderful effects of their art, laugh or cry, condemn or admire, love or hate, just as they please; subjugating the heart with every various passion: more especially when they pronounce the charms and incantations of a certain sorcerer, called Shakespeare, whose science was so powerful, that he himself thus describes it:

——————I have oft be-dimm'd
The noon-tide sun, call'd forth the mutinous
winds, &c."

CHAP. VI.

"Mr. Holcroft arrived in London, just at the time that Mr. Sheridan came into the management of Drury-Lane. He endeavoured to procure an engagement at this, and at the other house; but in vain. As a last desperate resource, when his money was nearly exhausted, he sat down and wrote a farce, called The Crisis, or Love and Famine, which Mrs. Sheridan was prevailed on to read; and this, with his musical knowledge (as he was able to sing in all choruses), procured him an engagement at twenty shillings a week. On his being engaged, Mr. Holcroft was desired by Mr. Sheridan to give in his cast of parts to Mr. Hopkins, the prompter; and they were as follow:

Don Manuel, . Kind Impostor.
Hardcastle, . She Stoops to Conquer.
Justice Woodcock, Love in a Village.
Hodge, ... Ditto.
Giles, ... Maid of the Mill.
Ralph, ... Ditto.
Sir Harry Sycamore, Ditto.

Scrub, ... Beaux' Stratagem.
Sir Anthony Absolute, Rivals.
General Savage, . School for Wives.
Colin Macleod, . Faithless Lover.
Mortimer, . . . Ditto.
Sir Benjamin Dove, Brothers.
Major O'Flaherty, . West-Indian.
Fulmer, ... Ditto.
Varland, ... Ditto.
Colonel Oldboy, Lionel and Clarissa.

It was in this last part that Mr. Holcroft particularly wished to have made his first appearance. The manner in which he procured a recommendation to Mrs. Sheridan, was through his cousin, Mrs. Greville. In consequence of this connexion, he also obtained introductions to Mrs. Crewe, and several other persons of fashion, who interested themselves in his behalf; and an epistolary intercourse commenced between him and Mr. Greville on subjects of taste and the theatre, which continued for some years.

His farce of the Crisis was, I believe, played but once, for the benefit of Hopkins, the prompter, when it was favourably received. This Mr. Hopkins, who had the regulation of the inferior parts in the theatre, entertained a very low opinion of Mr. Holcroft's powers as an actor; and he remained unnoticed, till Mr. Sheridan by chance saw him in the part of Mungo, with which he was so much pleased as to order his weekly salary to be raised to five and twenty shillings. Both his salary and his reputation in the theatre seem now to have remained stationary during this and the following season, though he constantly attended the theatre to perform the most menial parts. The following extract from a letter addressed to Mr. Sheridan, will sufficiently explain both his situation and feelings at this time:—

"Depressed, dejected, chained by Misfortune to the rock of Despair, while the vultures Poverty and Disappointment are feasting with increase of appetite upon me, I have no chance of deliverance but from you. You, Sir, I hope, will be my Alcides! Mr. Evans says, he must increase the deductions he already makes from my salary (9s. per week), unless I can obtain your order to the contrary. It is scarcely possible I should maintain my family, which will shortly be increased, upon my present income. Were I not under deductions at the office, my receipts would very little exceed sixty pounds a year; and this I enjoy more through your favour than any consequence I am of to the theatre, though continually employed. But then it is either to sit in a senate or at a card-table, or to walk in a procession, or to sing in a chorus, which is all that the prompter, who has the direction of this kind of business, thinks me capable of. Nay, in so little esteem am I held by Mr. Hopkins, that he took the part of a dumb steward in Love for Love from another person, and made me do it; and when by your permission I played Mawworm, he said, had he been well and up, it should not have been so. I do not mention this as a subject of accusation against Mr. Hopkins, but merely to shew that if I am consigned to his penetration, I am doomed to everlasting oblivion.

"Unhappily for me, when I performed Mawworm, you were not at the theatre. Interest rather than vanity makes me say, I was more successful than I had any reason to expect. The audience were in a continual laugh. I played Jerry Sneak for my own benefit last year, and with the same success; and if I could only be introduced to the town in old men and burletta singing, I know from former experience how soon I should be held in a very different estimation from what I am at present. You do not know, Sir, how useful I could be upon a thousand emergencies in the theatre, if I were but thought of; but this I shall never be till your express mandate is issued for that purpose.

"You have frequently been pleased to express a partiality towards me, as well as a favourable opinion of my abilities. But, sir, if you do not immediately interest yourself in my behalf, I may grow grey, while I enjoy your favour without a possibility of confirming or increasing it. 'Who's the Dupe' prevented the Crisis from being played last year; now you tell me you will talk to me after Christmas; in the mean time "the Flitch of Bacon" and a new pantomime are preparing. I told those to whom I am indebted, I should have a chance of paying them soon, for that the Crisis would come out before the holidays. When I said so, I believed that it would; but they will think I meant to deceive them."

The concluding sentence of this letter is remarkable, when we recollect the character of the celebrated man to whom it is addressed.

"In short, I am arrived at the labyrinth of delays, where suspense and all his busy imps are tormenting me—*You alone, Sir, hold the clue that can guide me out of it.*"

Mr. Sheridan, in spite of Mr. Holcroft's entreaties, was not inclined on this occasion to perform the part of Theseus; for he was still left to the mercy of the remorseless prompter, and had no opportunity of exerting his talents till the Camp came out (in 1780) when he endeavoured, as he expresses himself, *to make a part* of a foolish recruit, and succeeded; in consequence of which his salary was raised to thirty shillings weekly.

During the summer recesses of the years 1778 and 1779, Mr. Holcroft had not been idle, but had made excursions to the Canterbury, Portsmouth, and Nottingham theatres, where he moved in a higher range of parts, and escaped from the drudgery of choruses and processions. The state of his health appears to have been one inducement for his leaving town in 1779; for he says in a letter, dated from Nottingham, in June, that but for this consideration, he believes it would have been more profitable for him to have remained in London. In these excursions he seems to have established a pretty intimate correspondence with a Mr. Hughes, the Portsmouth or Plymouth manager; for we find the latter writing to him for a supply of performers, and Mr. Holcroft in answer complaining of his being able only to meet with a Mrs. Hervey, of whom he gives a very satirical portrait, and a Mr. Cubit, a singer, who, he observes, had already been with Mr. Hughes, and who never visited a company twice.

Mr. Holcroft's business at the theatre, did not hinder him from pursuing his literary avocations. Besides the Crisis, he had already written two other after-pieces, the Shepherdess of the Alps, and the Maid of the Vale.

The following letter to Mrs. Sheridan, gives an account of the first of these:

"Madam,

"It is with a peculiar pleasure that I have, by Mr. Sheridan's desire, an opportunity of addressing you. I am indebted to your benevolence and interposition, for my first obtaining admission in the theatre, and shall ever remember it with respect and gratitude. Give me leave, Madam, to intrude upon your patience for a moment, while I explain the motive of this address.—Mrs. Greville, Mrs. Crewe, and some other ladies of fashion and consequence, have kindly undertaken to patronize, and recommend the Shepherdess of the Alps. Mrs. Crewe has spoken to Mr. Sheridan concerning it, as he informed me last night, desiring me at the same time, to send it to you, who he said would not only read it yourself, but put him in mind of it. I believe myself almost certain of your good wishes, when you read the beginning, and recollect that your late dear and worthy brother pointed out the subject to me, encouraged me to pursue it, and had not only undertaken to set it, but had actually composed two songs. Pardon me, Madam, for introducing so melancholy a reflection. His esteem for me, I might almost say his friendship, shall never be forgotten, let my condition in life hereafter be what it may; it does me too much honour. You likewise, Madam, have some share in the work: it was in consequence of your advice and observations, that the comic part was introduced: it was at first intended only to affect the nobler passions, and to have been entirely serious. —I would not willingly appear too urgent: yet cannot forbear expressing some anxiety about the fate of my poor Shepherdess. I spent all the summer about it, (certain as I thought then) of its coming out immediately.

"I am, Madam," &c.

The Maid of the Vale was a translation from the Italian comic opera of La Buona Figliola, which Mr. Arne, the son of Dr. Arne, employed him to alter and adapt to the English stage.

A good deal of altercation seems to have taken place between the author and musician respecting the division of the future profits of the piece; Mr. Holcroft claiming one half, to which his employer did not think him by any means entitled. In consequence, I believe, of these disagreements, the piece was not brought forward.

Mr. Holcroft afterwards offered his translation of this opera to Mr. King, the late actor, at that time manager of Sadler's Wells, by whom it was rejected. Mr. Holcroft however, wrote several little pieces for Mr. King, which were brought out at this theatre. The Noble Peasant (which afterwards came out at the Haymarket,) was originally intended to have been acted here. Mr.

Holcroft always experienced from this gentleman the most liberal and friendly treatment, and was under considerable pecuniary obligations to him. Mr. Foote died in October, 1777, a few weeks before Mr. Holcroft came to town. In the spring of the following year, he published an Elegy on his Death, which was the first composition of his, that had appeared in print, (since his essays in the Whitehall Evening Post). It met with a favourable reception. He had always respected the character of Foote, had been personally known to him, and lamented his death in terms dictated by real feeling, as much as by the inspiration of the muse. At the same time, he published a short poem on Old Age, which was bound up with the elegy. In April, 1779, I find him desiring his father, who lived at Bath, to make inquiries respecting the prizes given at the Bath Easton Vase, the subjects proposed, and the length of the poems. "I have an inclination," he says, "to become a candidate for fame at that temple of Apollo, *not so much from a supposition that I shall gain the laurel, as because I think the plan deserves encouragement.*" The little deceptions of self-love, cannot but sometimes excite a smile.—It may be proper to notice here, that Mr. Holcroft kept up at this period a constant correspondence with his father, whose wife rented a small house and garden, either at or in the neighbourhood of Bath. The letters that passed between them, do honour to the feelings of both parties. Mr. Holcroft was always eager to communicate the news of any good fortune that had befallen him, and ready to lend every assistance in his power to his father, who was still frequently in pecuniary difficulties. From one of these letters, it appears that Mr. Holcroft, among other employments, had engaged to write a paper, called the Actor, for the Westminster Magazine, and that he was secretary to a society, (the theatrical fund,) for which he received ten pounds a year. He also found time to write songs for Vauxhall, several of which became very popular. Among these, the greatest favourite was the ballad, beginning, "Down the Bourne and through the Mead," which was set to music by Shield. This song, which is written in the Scottish dialect, has often been taken for an old Scotch ballad, and has been actually printed in a collection of Scotch songs.—Mr. Holcroft was one evening drinking tea with some friends at White-Conduit House, when the organ was playing the tune of Johnny and Mary. After they had listened some time, a person in the next box began to descant rather learnedly on the beauty of the Scotch airs, and the tenderness and simplicity of their popular poetry, bringing this very ballad as an illustration of his argument, neither the words nor music of which, he said, any one now living was capable of imitating. Mr. Holcroft on this, took occasion to remark the strange force of prejudice, and turning to the gentleman, interrupted his argument by informing him, that he himself was the author of the song in question, and that the tune was composed by his friend, Mr. Shield, who I believe was also there present.—This song had been composed for, and was originally sung at Vauxhall, by the celebrated Nan Catley. An Irish music-seller, at the St. Paul's Head in the Strand, had procured the words and music, and had advertised them in his window to be sold. Mr. Shield was accidentally passing, saw the music in the window, and went in to demand by what right the advertiser meant to publish his property. To this he received for answer, " By a very good right, for that the music was composed by him (the vender,) and that the words had been written by a friend, for Miss Catley, whom he very well knew." It was with difficulty that Mr. Shield by informing him that he was the author of the music, prevailed on the pretended composer to relinquish his claim.

Mr. Holcroft, almost on his coming to town, married his third wife; and soon after, she and Mr. Holcroft determined upon taking a small house, and furnishing it. They were, however, diverted from this plan by a Mr. Turner, an upholsterer, in Oxford Road, who persuaded them that it would be much more advantageous to take a large house, which he would furnish, and give them credit for any length of time they demanded. He said, that many persons by letting the upper part of their houses, not only cleared their rent, but were often gainers. These arguments, and the additional motive of making a more creditable appearance, induced Mr. Holcroft to take a house in Southampton Buildings, which Mr. Turner furnished as he had promised, to the value of 240l. But scarcely were the goods lodged in the house, before the upholsterer became a bankrupt, and his effects and bills were consigned over to his creditors, who immediately came on Mr. Holcroft for 160l. 80l. having been at first advanced to Mr. Turner for the furniture. This unexpected stroke completely ruined the prospects of our young house-keepers, and they were obliged to apply to several persons to prevent an execution, which was threatened. Mr. Holcroft might indeed have sold his goods for nearly the amount of the debt against him: but it seems that he was unwilling to see his property melt away under the hands of an auctioneer, and to have to begin the world again, after having, in a manner, realized all his hopes, by attaining a permanent and respectable establishment in life. He wrote to several persons to assist him in this emergency, with a degree of importunity which can only be excused by the severity of his disappointment, and a sense that it was undeserved on his part. He wrote to Mr. Greville, to a Mr. Laurel, to Mr. Sheridan, to the Proprietors of Drury-Lane, to persons whom he had never seen or known, with a kind of wild desperation. These applications indeed shewed no great knowledge of the world; but the abrupt appeals which he thus made to the humanity and generosity of others, at least proved that Mr. Holcroft was not without a strong sense of these qualities in his own breast, which made him believe they might be found to a romantic degree in others. His friend, Mr. King, at length relieved him from his immediate embarrassments by a loan of 80 or 100l. This, however, was to be repaid; and at no great distance of time, the same difficulties, and the same struggles to extricate himself from them returned. At one time, great hopes were entertained from the expected arrival of a Mr. Marsac, a near relation of his wife, who had a handsome appointment in India; and who, in their present situation, it was thought, would be willing to assist them. But he did not arrive within the time which had been fixed. Mr. Holcroft then wrote to a lady, high in rank and literary pretension, but a stranger to him, stating the circumstances of his case, and inclosing a comedy, which he had written as a voucher for the justice of his claims: she had been the laborious patroness of departed genius, and he thought might be the friend of living merit. But it seems, the inference was not justified by the event. The comedy was returned unread: and, indeed, if she had read it, a very favourable verdict could scarcely have been expected, under the annexed penalty of a hundred pounds. Mr. Holcroft has recorded this extravagance and its result among the adventures of Wilmot, the usher, in Hugh Trevor. Mr. Holcroft now looked forward, as a last resource, to the success of the comedy itself (Duplicity) which was afterwards acted with applause; but such was the author's untoward fate, that even his success was attended with little advantage, and relieved his necessities but in part.

Mr. Holcroft had, at this time, few friends or acquaintance in London, and those few were very little able to afford him any material assistance. The oldest were Shield and P——, both of whom he had known in strolling companies in the North: they had separated, had come to London about the same time, and met by chance. Shield first discovered Holcroft poring over an old book-stall, in Goodge-Street: they immediately recognized each other with a good deal of pleasure, and a friendly intercourse commenced, which was uninterrupted to the last. When the place of composer of the birth-day minuets at court became vacant by the death of Mr. Weideman, Mr. Holcroft applied to Mr. Greville to procure the place for Mr. Shield; with what success I do not know.

Mr. Shield at the period we are speaking of, had an engagement at the

Opera-house. It was winter, and in consequence of some new piece, they had very long rehearsals every morning. One day he was detained longer than usual, his dinner-hour was over, he felt himself very cold when he came out, and his attendance for so many hours had sharpened his appetite. He therefore proceeded up the Hay-market with a determination to get some refreshment at the first place that offered. He had strolled into St. Martin's-lane, without meeting with any thing that he liked: till he came to a little bye-court, called Porridge Island; at the corner of which, in a dark, dirty-looking window, he discovered a large round of beef smoking, which strongly seconded the disposition he already felt in himself to satisfy his hunger. He did not, however, much like the appearance of the place: he looked again, the temptation grew stronger, and at last he ventured in. Having asked for dinner, he was shewn into a room up one pair of stairs, not very large, but convenient and clean, where he found several persons already set down to dinner. He was invited to join them, and to his great joy found both the fare and the accommodation excellent. But his attention was shortly much more powerfully arrested by the conversation which took place at the table. Philosophy, religion, politics, poetry, the belles lettres were talked of, and in such a manner, as to shew that every person there was familiar with such subjects, and that they formed the ordinary topics of conversation. Mr. Shield listened in a manner which denoted his surprise and pleasure. The conversation at one time began to take rather a free turn, when a grave, elderly looking man, who sat at the head of the table, addressed the new guest, telling him that he seemed a young man, and by his countenance shewed some signs of grace; that he would not have him mind what was said by persons who scarcely believed their own sophisms; that he himself when young had been attacked and staggered by the same objections; that he had examined them all, and found them all false and hollow. This diverted the discourse to other subjects which were more agreeable. The name of the person who had thus addressed Mr. Shield, and who thus assumed the office of a censor, was Cannon: he was the son of an Irish bishop. He was advanced in years, and presided in the company with an air of authority that was partly submitted to in earnest, and partly humoured for the joke's sake. He regularly dined here every day.

On entering the room, he first pulled off his great coat, and fastened it with two long pins to the back of a tall cane-worked old chair with knobs behind: and after disposing of his umbrella, which in those days was a great singularity, he used to pay his respects to the company with much formality, and then sat down. He had one place, which was always kept for him; and for this privilege it seems he paid double price. If any stranger came in by chance, and took possession of his seat, he would never sit down in any other, but walked up and down the room in a restless way, till the person was gone. It was his constant custom to carry with him a small pocket volume of Milton, or Young's Night Thoughts, in which he had made a great number of marginal notes; and as soon as dinner was over, he regularly took out one of his favourite authors, and opening the book at random, requested the person who sat next him, whether a stranger, or one of the usual company, to read aloud a certain passage which he thought very beautiful. This offer was of course declined by those who knew him, who in return begged that he would favour the company with it himself, which he did, at the same time repeating the remarks which he had made in the margin. He then very deliberately closed the book, and put it into his pocket again. Cannon was a man of letters, and had travelled. He spoke a very florid language, full of epithets and compound words, and professed to be engaged in an edition of Tibullus. Mr. Shield was so much amused with this old gentleman, and interested in the general conversation, (not to say that the commons were excellent), that he was determined he would in future dine no where else:

he was also eager to inform Holcroft of the discovery he had made, whom he invited to go along with him the next day, and who also became a very constant visitor. The persons who were generally present were Messieurs Shield, Nicholson, Holcroft, Cannon, &c., who formed themselves into a little society, which in compliment to the last mentioned person, was called "The Cannonian." The president was rather tenacious of his opinions, and impatient of contradiction; and frequently some very warm altercations took place in consequence between him and Mr. Holcroft.

The other friend of Mr. Holcroft, mentioned above, was a young Scotchman, who had been in Booth's company with him, but soon quitted it, and came up to London two or three years before him. They had had a violent quarrel while they were in this company, but meeting again in London, with new objects before them, and where they were both to a considerable degree strangers, former disagreements were forgotten, and a friendly intercourse commenced. He strenuously advised Holcroft to turn his thoughts to writing, or reporting for the newspapers, which he himself had found a lucrative employment, which Holcroft declined, being more bent on pushing his way at the theatre.

The manner in which this friend of our author began his career in life, deserves a place in a work which is little else than a history of the difficulties and successes which attend the efforts of men of talents and literature.

Mr. P——, whose connexions were respectable, came to town, with recommendations to a banking-house in the city, and with an intention to get a place as clerk in some counting-house, or public office. He delivered his letters, and his friends promised they would be on the look-out for him. He called once or twice to no purpose, and as his time hung rather idly on his hands, he had employed himself in writing one or two anonymous letters on the politics of the day, which were inserted in the General Advertiser. It so happened that one of the partners in the house to which he had been recommended, had a principal share in this very paper: and when he called, he told him that he had heard of nothing in the way that he wished; but taking out the Advertiser, and shewing him his own letter in it, "If now," said he, "you could do something of this kind, I might possibly be of service to you." Mr. P—— replied, with some eagerness, that he was the author of the letter. "Aye, indeed," says the other, "then come with me; we must have some farther talk together." So saying, he took our young politician with him into another room; and after being closeted some time, it was arranged that P—— should be immediately employed as a writer and reporter for this paper, at a guinea and half a week. The very next night there was to be an important debate in the house, and our young gentleman was to make his *coup d'essai*. As however he was entirely ignorant of the forms and rules of reporting, it was thought necessary to give him some previous instructions; and he was told, that he should place himself so as to be able to hear the speakers distinctly; that he should provide himself with a pencil and pocket-book, in which he must note down the speeches as privately as he could; but that as he was a stranger, and might be noticed the more on that account, if any one came to interrupt him, he was to say nothing, but put half a guinea into his hand. Thus equipped and instructed,

Mr. P—— went early to his post, and planted himself in the middle of the gallery, directly in front of the speaker. He had his pencil and pocket-book ready in his hand, and the instant the debate opened, began to take notes with so much eagerness, and so little precaution, that a messenger came to him, and said, "Sir, you must give over writing." As he had been prepared for this event, he took the half guinea out of his pocket, and bending his hand behind him, offered the half-guinea, which was lodged in the palm of it, to the door-keeper, who took it without saying a word, and the other went on with his writing as before. But no sooner had he begun, than the man very quietly tapped him on the shoulder again, and said, "Sir, you must give over writing." This second rebuff was quite unexpected, and completely disconcerted our zealous reporter. He put his pencil and paper in his pocket, and sat during the remainder of the debate in a state of the utmost confusion, not expecting to remember a single sentence. He went home and related his ill-success; professing his inability to give any account of what he had heard. "But," said his employer, "you may at least try: you must surely recollect something of what passed." He said, "no: he had been in such a state of agitation the whole time, that it would be in vain to attempt it." As no one else had gone from the same office, and it was absolutely necessary to give some account of the debate the next morning, he was again urged to make the attempt, and at length complied. He was left in the room by himself, and scarcely knowing what he did, began an account of the speech of Lord Nugent, who had opened the question. He was surprised to find that he could recollect the few first sentences. Still he despaired of being able to proceed: but by degrees, one thing recalled another, he still kept writing on without knowing what was to follow, and when he had finished one page, sent it down to the press. His hopes now began to revive, he returned to the charge, and writing under an apprehension that the words might every minute escape from his memory, he despatched sheet after sheet so vigorously, that the press could hardly keep pace with him. They had now printed two columns and a half, and Lord Nugent was still speaking. At last, the proprietor, who had at first dreaded a dearth of information, and whose fears were now alarmed the contrary way, came up to him, and said, "My G—d, when will this Lord Nugent's speech be done? Was there no other speaker the whole evening?" "Oh yes, there are seven or eight more to come." The other laughed, and told P—— that he had quite mistaken the business; that in his way of going on, he would fill a volume instead of a newspaper, and that he must begin again entirely, and instead of giving every word and sentence, merely repeat the heads of each speech, and a few of the most striking arguments. "Oh, is that all you want," exclaimed P——, at once relieved from his terrors, "then I'm your man." Accordingly he set to work afresh, cut down Lord Nugent into half a column, and the other speakers had a proportionable space allotted them: and the report, thus curtailed, was the next day noticed as the ablest and fullest that had been given of the debate. The person, to whom this anecdote relates, has been long known to the public as the editor and proprietor of the only constitutional paper that remains.

END OF THE FIRST VOLUME.

J. M'Creery, Printer,
Black Horse Court, Fleet Street London

www.ingramcontent.com/pod-product-compliance
Lightning Source LLC
Chambersburg PA
CBHW050715100426
42735CB00041B/3190
* 9 7 8 1 5 3 5 8 0 7 2 9 6 *